Chopper

Mark Brandon Read

JOHN BLAKE

Published by John Blake Publishing Ltd,
3 Bramber Court, 2 Bramber Road, London W14 9PB, England

First published in paperback in Great Britain in 2002

ISBN 1 903402 39 5

British Library Cataloguing-in-Publication Data:
A catalogue record for this book is available from
the British Library.

Typeset by t2

Printed and bound in Great Britain by
Bookmarque Ltd, Croydon, Surrey

18 20 19

Contents

Form No. **260**

Fingerprint—Records Section,
Information Bureau,
Police Headquarters,
Melbourne 55

| Fingerprint Classification | 5/17 U/U 000/000 23/17 | | Date | 4th February, 1975. |

Photo Book Numbers: Gaol photo 75-138/78 Gaol Photo 75-138/83:
Gaol Photo 5197 (71): Gaol Photo 75/130/76 VGP.376/77 VGP.46/78

| I.B.R. No. | L.R.720 | Docket No. | 3337/74 | Gaol No. | CRN 3403 |

Date of birth 17.11.1954. Record of Convictions against READ: Mark Brendon.
@ Jack Read. @ Mark Brandon Read. @ "CHOPPER READ MARK".

Court		Date			Offence	Sentence
VICTORIA. Melbourne	C.C.	18	5	71	Attempted Storebroom break & steal	Admitted to S.W.B. as Mark Brendon Read.
Ringwood	M.C.	20	12	71	Assault by kicking.) Unlawful assault) (2 charges).) Indecent language.	1 month on each charge. $10 def. 2 days. as Mark Brandon Read.
Lilydale	M.C.	24	5	74	Armed with offensive weapon.	1 month. as Mark Brendon Read.
Melbourne	M.C.	26	11	74	Indecent language. Assault Police (2 charges).	$50 def. distress. 1st charge Adjourned for 2 years on a $50 G.B. Bond. 2nd charge Struck Out. as Mark Brandon Read.
Elsternwick	M.C.	18	4	75	Burglary.) Assault.) Impersonate police.)	6 months. 2 months on each charge concurrent & concurrent with 1st charge.as Mark Brandon Read.
Melbourne County Court		1	5	75	Burglary with intent to commit assault occasioning actual bodily harm. Rape. Robbery in company.	Acquitted by direction. Acquitted. 2 years.Minimum 15 month as Mark Brandon Read.
Visiting Pentridge	M.C.	11	2	76	Attempt escape. Absent from place of recreation. Possess articles not issued.	2 months. 1 month conct. 1 month. as Mark Brandon Read.
Melbourne County Court		1	12	75	Armed robbery in company.	12 months.as Mark Brandon Read.
Melbourne	M.C.	31	5	77	Breach of Probation of 26.11.74.	Probation cancelled.1 month concurrent with current sentence.

Chapter 1

Digging my Own Grave

'I'd lived with murder contracts over my head for years.'

I have been shot once, stabbed seven times, had a claw hammer stuck in my skull, been run over, beaten unconscious and left for dead. Any one of those incidents could have killed me. But the time I came closest to dying didn't leave me with any scars at all. Except, maybe, on my soul. I still dream about it sometimes.

It is something I have never told anyone. It happened one night in 1977, when I went for a walk to the shops in South Yarra.

I'd lived with murder contracts over my head for years. Most of the best crooks in Australia have wanted me dead, so I should have known better than to drop my guard and wander around the suburbs like a tourist.

I was taken by total suprise. I was walking along the street when a man jumped out of his car and began to look at a road map on the bonnet. He had a torch on the map and looked puzzled. He called me over and asked if I knew where a certain street was. Not suspecting a thing, I looked at the map …

He had a gun under the map. In the split-second that I saw the barrel shining in the torchlight as he swung it up, I knew it was too late. He had it under my neck. Seconds later, I was in the boot of his Monaro, handcuffed.

It is a matter of shame and embarrassment that I could have been so stupid to get captured so easily. I'd been put in the boot with an old trick.

The abductor was a Melbourne criminal who I will not name. It's funny what you remember. He had the car cassette player on and was listening to Dean Martin's greatest hits. That music still makes me feel sombre now. You can't imagine the terror. I can still almost taste the petrol and exhaust fumes I smelt on that ride. I could hear the tyres spread as we went over tram tracks, presumably the ones in Toorak Road.

I hadn't suspected for a moment that it could have been a set-up, even though he was parked and waiting for me to get near the car before he jumped out to look at the map. It was my fault. But I didn't give up hope. I vowed that would be my only mistake that night.

After all, the enemy had already made one mistake, too – not finishing me when he had the chance. I was willing the car to stop so that I could get back on my feet. I didn't know whether he planned to torture me or whether it would be straight-out murder. I thought I had smelt alcohol on his breath when I was trying to read the road map so I hoped he was a little pissed. Anything which would slow his reflexes down to give me an outside chance.

My mind was racing at 1000 miles an hour and I decided that the first half chance I had, I would go for it. I knew that without a bit of luck there would be no tomorrow. While I was thinking and trying to plan, all I could hear was Dean Martin blasting out 'Everybody Loves Somebody Sometime'. I couldn't help laughing a little at the song, considering my circumstances. I would have loved a few friends, all armed to the teeth.

I was full of terror at the thought of what was going to happen. But I kept thinking, 'He's made one mistake already by not killing me; if he makes another I might have a chance.'

He had handcuffed me with my hands at the front. I thought about trying to kick my way out of the boot, but it would have made too much noise. One bullet through the back seat would have finished me.

He pulled me out of the boot. As soon as he hit me with the pistol butt, I knew it wasn't going to be a straight shooting: I was in for the flogging first. I was beaten, kicked, pistol whipped and punched. It was the first time and only time I'd ever lost control of my bowels through fear. But the pain was nothing ... at least I was still alive.

The bashing over, it was stage two. He marched me through the dark about 30 feet in front of the car and handed me a garden spade.

I had to dig my own grave.

I think he was surprised I didn't argue, but started digging straight away.

After a while I complained I couldn't dig properly with handcuffs on, and he unlocked them.

That was his second mistake.

I dug as hard as I could, and all the time I was talking to him, laughing and making stupid jokes. I was digging like a mad Welsh coal miner. I know my vigour in digging put him off guard.

All the time this was happening I didn't allow my face to reflect the terror I felt. I laughed and joked about the predicament I was in while digging the hole. The bloke said: 'You're a tough bastard, Chopper. I'll give you that.'

That compliment – and the word 'No!' – were the last words he spoke.

When I was about hip deep in the grave, I could sense he felt it was deep enough. I had to do something – anything to buy a bit more time. I pretended I had hit a hard spot. I took a fresh grip on the handle of the spade with my left hand as if I was going to dig even harder.

I am right-handed but he was standing on my left side above me. I gripped the shovel like a baseball bat – and let go at his left kneecap.

I knew he would get a shot off. But it was the only card I had left, and I had to play it. A wounded man, a man with the blade of a spade through his kneecap, wouldn't be taking correct aim.

I also know my guns. He had a Spanish-made, very heavy, cheap .45 calibre automatic, and after banging me about the head with it, who knows? It might jam on him.

So I took the chance and swung. He screamed in pain and fired. The flash of the gun was right beside my head. I was going to die anyway, so I had nothing to lose. I nearly severed his leg with that first blow.

Next second, I was out of the grave. That's when he screamed, 'No!'.

For him, it was too late. The spade was in his brain.

Let's say, for me it was a bit of a character builder.

That night still chills me to the bone. I don't feel as though I defeated a worthy opponent. I simply cheated death.

I got into the car. It was more comfortable to be in the driver's seat than the boot. I drove along the track and found a main road. It was only then, when I found a sign, that I realised my last resting place was to have been Mount Donna Buang, up past Warburton. I drove the car home. The other bloke didn't need it. He was in the ground.

While I had been putting him in the grave, I kept thinking I could hear a man walking through the bush. It was probably a wild pig, but it sounded spooky. Let me tell you that if it was a man, he did himself a big favour by not coming over to say hello. There was plenty of room for two in that hole.

Being ordered to dig my own grave is something I try to forget, and I have never talked about it. I got out alive because of the other chap's lack of concentration and because I kept cool. I was looking at my own death that night; it still comes back in my dreams sometimes.

I remember standing over his body that night and saying, 'Thank you, God.' I believe that God must have protected me that night.

He was good. He had got me and beaten me fair and square, and full credit to him. He may have been a bit pissed but he taught me a lot that night, about what to do and what not to do. Nevertheless, he got me and the fact that I lived and he died doesn't count.

I was a dead man. He had me cold, so why he went through the drama of getting me to dig the grave I wouldn't know. I have heard that quite a few fellows in the 1970s had to dig their own graves but none of them got a second chance. The bloke who got me was as stupid as he was clever.

I've dug a few graves in my time. But I have never made a man dig his own. There's no need to go that far – it would be plain bad manners.

I was walking to the shops when the would-be hitman got me. The moral is simple: never go to the shops without your gun.

When you have killed a man the brain sometimes fuzzes over the details. The mind numbs itself, otherwise anyone who has ever killed would end up in a mental hospital.

I remember waking up the next morning and thinking for a moment, 'Did that really happen?' Then I looked in the mirror and saw all the lumps and cuts on my head from the pistol whipping, and I knew it was for real.

People now think I am mad because I don't show physical

fear, but after that night what is there to frighten me? How can the police, the prisons, the screws, courts, judges or criminal world frighten anyone who has stood in his own grave – and lived?

There may be some who doubt the story. Well, I am quite prepared to do a full re-enactment for them, providing they ride in the boot. I'll even bring the Dean Martin tape.

There were other times when I should have died. Plenty of them. In 1977 I was attacked and beaten nearly to death by two Melbourne criminals armed with baseball bats outside a pub in Port Melbourne. They only left when they thought I was dead. The two criminals, who I will not name, are no longer with us.

I was hit by a car in a hit and run in 1974 and left lying unconscious in a South Yarra street, I never found out who was behind that attempt.

I was beaten half to death in the toilets of the old Dover Hotel in the city by a group of criminals. I'm still not 100 per cent sure who was behind that, although I have been trying to find out for years.

I hate talking about defeats and near-defeats. But, oh well, what the hell.

I think I should say that I have shot, wounded and crippled 11 men altogether. One chap lost an arm, one wears a colostomy bag, one lost his leg, one has a badly-crippled leg, one has a pin in his hip, another a pin in his shoulder, one lost an eye and has brain damage. And the rest have life-time gut aches.

But they are at least alive, if not well.

I think I was 17 or 18 when I shot my first man. I used to shoot people in the feet and legs when I was younger but I don't count them. Who counts a little .22 slug?

As for killing, I can't be charged for simply saying that I've killed more than one man. I don't know if anyone will believe me but I will tell the truth about the past.

If you combine the deaths I have carried out personally, those I've been involved in with helpers and partners, and the deaths I have helped plan but not taken any personal part in, the figure is quite large. I have no worries about acting as a 'consultant', then leaving others to carry out the dirty work. If you can make a monkey dance then grind the organ, I say. The upshot is that, either personally, in company, or at a distance, I have been involved in 19 deaths inside and outside jail since 1971. OK, it's no world record, but it's not bad for the little kid in the schoolyard who always got bashed.

All those who died had it coming. There wasn't a 'civilian' in the bunch, and I don't regret one. It's not that many when you think of all the criminal violence there has been in Victoria over the years.

Strange as it may seem, I have never considered myself a murderer, because they all had it coming. Most of them came under the heading of tactical necessities. All of them were killers and violent crims, so big deal.

I have never felt that I murdered, or helped out in anyone's murder. I always believed that the 'Dear Departed' had it coming in the eyes of God. One drug dealer I killed – as a matter of fact, he died of shock half-way through a kneecapping – had bragged of overdosing about 50 prostitutes and junkies over a ten-year period in the western suburbs. How could his death be classed as murder?

Consider that. Fifty people. God, I'm just a babe in arms. One out of every three drug overdoses is a hotshot. Some of the chaps I've grabbed were mass murderers in the drug world. Compared with them, I'm no murderer ... I'm a garbage disposal expert.

What Julian Knight did at Hoddle Street, that was murder. I have never killed an innocent member of the community.

Just as a point of interest, every man that I have shot or stabbed, who lived, looked up at me like a beaten puppy and asked, 'Why?' Before a man dies, his last word always seems to be 'No'.

Men from certain ethnic groups cry and scream and go to their deaths like screaming females, crying, 'No, No, No.'

The hardest man of all, without a shadow of a doubt, was an old Scot from Glasgow. He was an old crook and as hard as nails. Even after two burnt feet from a blowtorch he didn't let out a scream or a tear; he just abused and spat blood on us. He was tied up and secured, but feared nothing. He knew he was going to die, but struggled and fought, yelled abuse and spat.

In the end, he gave nothing. We shot him to shut him up. He was a tough fearless bastard, and we had to admire him. Reluctantly, I have to admit the mad Scot came from Sydney to

Melbourne. He would be the only tough man to come out of Sydney, in my opinion.

The smell when you put a blowtorch to someone's feet is hard to describe. It is a cross between burnt hair and roast pork. A sweet, sickly smell that hangs heavily in the air and gets right into your hair and clothing.

I still have a few mixed feelings about some of the things that I have written. Telling normal people some of the things I have done makes me feel ill at ease. Violence, death, guns and torture has been my whole life for so long now, it seems normal to me, inside and outside jail.

That is all I seem to talk about and think about, or involve myself in. How many people that a person has killed in his life is a question that is never asked in the criminal world and would never be answered at any rate. I don't think I can get into trouble, I've named no one: no name, no murder. But it still leaves me with mixed feelings. I've done enough jail.

None of the people I've killed were innocent, normal or average nine-to-five working types: they were all drug dealers, hoons, pimps, crime figures and killers. I doubt whether any one of them was a virgin as far as death and murder were concerned. Some of them had killed plenty in the drug world with a needle.

I have a clear heart and clear mind over it all, but I've never come out and put a number on it before. I know this sounds quite odd, but I still suffer from confused religious beliefs as a result of my upbringing. I suffer no real guilt but I know that in the eyes of God even killing scum is wrong. But then again He's let me live and let them die.

However, writing about these things gives me a nagging inner discomfort. I can't put a finger on it. I guess my strict Seventh Day Adventist upbringing is coming back to haunt me.

Every now and again I suffer bouts of bad conscience, a type of guilt left over from my upbringing. I am by no means a religious man, but the teachings of childhood are hard to shake off. It may come as a shock to those who know me but I do feel spooky at times about some of the things that I have done. I justify it all to myself by saying that I've never killed or hurt anybody who didn't have it coming to them in the eyes of God. But sometimes I get spooked as none of us knows what awaits us in the hereafter. Personally, I think I am owed an apology.

Anyone who has killed will confess in private that the faces of his victims come back in his dreams. I have spoken to multiple murderers like Robert Wright and Julian Knight about this. In Knight's case it is not the faces but the whole Hoddle Street massacre that comes back.

Quite a few fellows who have taken human life have confessed to me in private that I am not the only one who has this happen to them. Every now and again the buggers come back to you in your dreams and talk to you. In my case, it has been quite disturbing over the years.

Anyone who has killed and claims the face or the event does not come back to them in a dream is lying.

It is no secret that mental health and myself have enjoyed a shaky friendship at times, but at the risk of being called a nutcase, I will admit that I believe in God. It may sound silly, but I used to pray before going into battle. I used to have a silent prayer, 'Lord, if you are with me, no man can stand against me.'

Having escaped death so many times has only strengthened my belief. I believed that The Lord saw my enemies as foul sinners and me as his messenger sent to punish them. I no longer believe that. But if there is no God then I am the luckiest man to have survived all the battles. It is something I often think about.

Perhaps I am alive because as bad as I am, The Lord saw me as the lesser of two warring evils and allowed my enemies to die or be defeated.

Who knows what is the truth? I have lived through too many attempts to kill me for it to be simply good fortune or my own quick thinking.

At my murder trial, I prayed to God to make the jury find me not guilty. You figure it out. I can't.

They say there are no atheists in foxholes, and I have stood at the edge of the grave for most of my life. It is hard for me not to wonder, at times, why I am still alive. How have I continued to escape death in every life and death situation?

I don't ever talk about this stuff inside jail. People in here think I am mad enough already without adding to it. But I can't help thinking, if God was not with me, why am I alive? No one has that much luck on his own.

Chapter 2

From Orphanage to Pentridge

'Don't ask for mercy from a man who has been shown no mercy.'

THE name 'Read' is an old Irish name. I've been told that 'Reid' is English and 'Reed' is Scottish. The name Brandon, my middle name, comes from Brandon Head, a small fishing village on the south west coast of Ireland in the county of Kerry.

I was born in Carlton on November 17, 1954. I spent the first 18 months of my life in the Methodist Babies Home in Melbourne, in which time my sister Debbie was born.

My mum's name is Valerie, and Dad's is Keith. Mum was an ultra-strict Seventh Day Adventist. Dad became a Seventh Day Adventist to marry Mum.

To be honest my mum and I were never close. The church ruled her life. It came before family, before everything. Mum told Dad to get out when I was 16 years old. They divorced when I was 19.

I hated the Seventh Day Adventist Church. I had a violent childhood, and I was sort of 'brainwashed'. I didn't feel loved as a kid and I grew up praying to God that He would kill my mother. I loved my dad, although he belted hell out of me as a child right up until I fought him back at the age of 15. Every time my dad belted me it was at my mum's orders.

I ran away from home six times between the age of 10 and 15. It was not a happy time for me, but I don't blame the past for what I am.

My grandfather, Mum's father, was a Seventh Day Adventist minister, Pastor George Weslake. I hated the church and I hated my home life, and it gives me no joy to remember it. But I do love my old dad. He left the church when I was 15 or 16, after I stopped going to church.

I don't remember ever liking my sister Debbie. To this day she is a devout Christian. She left the Seventh Day Adventists to become a born-again Christian. She sends me letters telling me to change my evil ways – or else burn in the fires of Hell.

As a cook my mum would have made a great steam cleaner. Everything I ate was either steamed or boiled. By the time I left home at 15 to go cane cutting up north I was practically steamed and boiled.

There is a saying: 'Don't ask for mercy from a man who has been shown no mercy.' As a kid I was shown no mercy, so I'd rather not go into much detail about my childhood. My best and happiest days have been on the streets of Melbourne. If I had happy times at all it would be when my dad moved us to Mornington for a couple of years. They were carefree days. There was still violence in the home but I loved Mornington.

The seaside was wonderful. When I settle down for good I'd love to live by the seaside.

One of the few things about my childhood that was completely normal was that, like most kids, I had a dog, which I loved. One day there was a blow-up at home. Dad walked out, and naturally I followed. When things were patched up Cindy was nowhere to be found. She had been put to sleep. I don't think I'll ever forget that.

I was put into Melbourne mental hospitals a few times when I was about 15, but my dad got me out. I was put into assorted mental institutions up until I was 19, but dad kept getting me out. I was given several treatments of deep-sleep therapy. My mother thought I was dyslexic and autistic. The fact was all I was really guilty of was leaving the Seventh Day Adventist Church.

I was treated for all manner of mental disorders. Some in my family were convinced that my rejecting the Seventh Day Adventist Church showed that I had a severe mental disorder and that it had to be treated. Of course, my treatment back in the mental hospitals in those days was not kind.

I was sent to a mental hospital in the south-eastern suburbs of Melbourne where I underwent deep-sleep therapy. I was completely off my head when I got out of one of the mental hospitals. I was put in assorted institutions four times as a teenager.

It took about ten years for me to get over the so-called treatments I got. I was completely psychopathic when I got out of there once. They put me on all sorts of weird and wonderful drugs and shock treatment. With the shock treatment they put the big bit in your mouth and hold you down and give you a big charge of the soup. I used to have a saying, 'EST won't get me.'

It was terrifying as a teenager to be placed in a ward with grown men strapped to their beds. The noise was unbelievable.

I know it's popular these days to talk about all the abuse you got as a child. Personally I'd rather keep the worst parts to myself. That's my business. But some of it would make strong men vomit, if I told all. I'll leave it at that. I suppose it could have been worse. Mum could have taken me on a day trip to Ayers Rock. Ha ha.

My childhood and schooldays were nothing to talk about, except that all I ever learnt as a child and teenager was violence and hatred for would-be tough guys.

In my schooldays in the 1960s I was the victim of schoolyard bullies five days a week. There were fights in the schoolyard day in, day out, and Adventists tend to get picked on. I must have been the most punished kid at any school I went to. Six of the best on each hand.

I grew up to hate bullies. I guess that's why I take such delight in belting the hell out of the so-called 'tough guys'. I'm violent, but I'm not a bully. Everyone I've ever moved against has been a bully boy, a two-bob tough guy. Most of the truly violent men I've known in my life have been the victims of school bullies and violence in the home.

I took a twisted pride in the fact I was the most strapped kid at school. I remember once I was kicked so bad in the head by bullies at Lalor High School that my parents didn't recognise me at first when I got home. But I always came back for more. Every time I got knocked down, I got up – for more, and more, and more, again and again.

As I said, through the 60s I ran away from home six times. One adventure was going into the city on the train when I was a 10-year-old to see the Beatles. I never did get to see the Beatles, but I had a great time getting lost in the crowds.

Another time I ran off to see LBJ, the American president, with other kids in front of the town hall. After kicking my way through the crowd to try to shake hands with him, I got to see the paint splashed over one of the cars. It was a great adventure.

I used to love to go in and watch the anti-war marches. The other kids and me would stand on the footpath and spit and yell abuse at the anti-war protesters. The whole city seemed to be closed and empty. Everyone was either marching or yelling abuse at the marchers. It was all high adventure for a young teenager.

I remember in 1969 going to see a then little-known lady in the city at some shopping centre place. She kissed me on the cheek and got lipstick all over me ... it was Edna Everage, now Dame Edna Everage. Silly old drag queen.

The 60s was a great time for kids to grow up. When Harold Holt died I remember there were big posters all over Melbourne – photos of Holt with the words 'A Great Australian' written underneath. A lot of Australian history happened in the 60s. It was a good time.

When I was growing up Australia was still influenced by the

White Australia policy. We hated all 'wogs' ... yet my girlfriend Margaret, the greatest chick I've ever known, is Maltese. We hated all 'Abos', yet I've been shown great kindness by Aborigines. We hated all Asians yet – and I've never told anyone this – my Dad is quarter caste Chinese. Their family name was Shan Han, but later they changed it to Shanhan to give it a more Irish sound.

Looking at my dad it is very hard to pick that he is quarter Chinese. He hates the Japs. Everyone I've ever met born in this country – regardless of their race or family nationality – is racist towards some other race or nationality or culture.

Whites in Australia either hate the blacks or the 'slopes' – or, if not, they don't mind a sly giggle at their expense. In years to come the Asians in Australia – talking with Aussie accents and drinking beer in the pubs and going to the footy – will be putting shit on the 'wogs' and 'coons', as the 'wogs' and blacks are already putting shit on the 'chows' and 'slopes'.

I don't think it is really blood-hatred racism but more a part of the 'rough as guts' Australian sense of humour, part of the Aussie culture and attitude.

Anyway, I'm racist – and my great-granny was a chow, bless her heart.

My mum's father fought in the First World War in the cavalry, but I don't know much about him. My dad's father, Alfred Read, was nicknamed 'The Bull' because of his great physical strength. He could bend a penny in half between his thumb and forefinger. He fought bare knuckles as a heavyweight prize fighter and worked as a shearer, wool presser and horseman. He was once photographed at Dalgety's wool stores with a bale of wool weighing 900 pounds resting on his shoulders as it was being rolled from platform to truck.

After the First World War, 'Bull' Read bought and sold remount horses – travelling with them to India, where he would do the deal. He walked out on my dad and his young brother and my grandmother when Dad was a small boy. My grandma died in Dad's arms when he was about 14. Dad worked as a stockman then joined the army at 16 to find that his father 'Alf the Bull' had also joined up for the Second World War.

Dad did a bit of boxing in the army. That's where he first met his good friend Eddy Miller. Later, I used to call Eddy Miller 'Uncle Eddy'. He was a great old chap. When my dad took us to live in Mornington in the 60s for two years Uncle Eddy had a taxi cab business down there. It was down there that Eddy and Dad taught me to box when I was a kid.

As a teenager I was always interested in joining the army. I did try to enlist once but got knocked back because I failed the psychiatric test ... the female captain psychiatrist said I had a personality given to violence.

Using that as an excuse to stop someone joining the army – well, I thought it was quite amusing. I admit, I also had flat feet, but I didn't get as far as the medical.

In 1977 when I got out of prison, with my dad's help and on his advice, I applied to join the Rhodesian Security Forces. I wrote away to the head of the forces – a Major General Kurt something or other. As I expected, I was accepted, and the necessary application forms plus assorted other paper work and travel instructions arrived. I filled out the application form and sent it back. A letter returned to say I had to fly to South Africa and then take a bus up to Salisbury, Rhodesia, as you couldn't fly from Australia to Rhodesia direct.

I told the Parole Board via my parole officer that I was leaving. 'No, you aren't,' said the parole officer. 'You're on parole; you're going nowhere.' Had I been allowed to leave we wouldn't be bothering with all this now, and the Victorian Government would have saved a fortune in jail and courts, police and legal costs.

Some men dream of dying in a hail of bullets, and in 1977 I was one of those men. But my dream was not to be. You could die of old age and boredom in Melbourne if you were hoping to die in a hail of gunfire in face-to-face combat in the streets. Let's face it, the Australian crim isn't a great one for any form of gun-in-hand face-to-face shoot-it-out combat. If they ever get me, it will be in the back.

When I ran away to Queensland when I was a teenager I worked for a while on the canefields in Mossman, 40 miles north of Cairns in Queensland. One day I caught a skinny black snake about two feet long. I had no idea what it was, and still don't – I'm no snake expert. But it was handy.

I was having some bother with some Abo cane cutters, so I held the snake around my neck and said, 'Come on.' They backed away, so it must have been a nice, evil type of snake.

I emptied the hut real quick the night I brought 'Speedy' back from the canefield. I fed him live mice. He would eat two a week. He didn't seem to drink, and he would cough his mouse bones and muck up the day after he'd eaten. I lasted a month on the canefields – cane toads, snakes, 100-degree heat, dirt and sweat – chopping cane by hand for $35 a bloody week. It was twice as much as a 15-year-old was paid in 1970, but I didn't like sleeping in a hut with farting, snoring, drunken cane cutters.

I brought my snake back to Melbourne and swapped him for a carpet snake and a python. Boy, did I have fun with them. I would push the face of the carpet snake into the faces of my enemies while my friends Dave the Jew and Cowboy Harris held them. The carpet snake would bite down. You could pick my enemies around Prahran – we moved from Thomastown to Prahran in 1970 – as a fair few of them had badly swollen and festering faces from the bite of the carpet snake.

The carpet snake and the python were called Reggie and Ronnie after the Kray brothers in London. The Krays had been my boyhood heroes, and I'd read that they, too, had kept pet snakes.

My teenage gang was made up of Terry the Tank, Dave the Jew and Cowboy Johnny Harris. We were the Surrey Road gang. We hung around at the Try Boys youth club with Lee and Wade Dix – Billy Dix's boys. I did Greco-Roman wrestling, swimming, and weightlifting and I boxed at Ambrose Palmer's gym in West Melbourne. I used to wrestle with big Lee Dix. He is now a top nightclub bouncer and still a good mate of mine.

Try Boys youth club was our headquarters. We had a collection of iron bars, knives, sawn-off shotguns and .22 calibre rifles, tomahawks, and meat cleavers. With 'Ronny and Reggie' in their carry bag we were a young but violently advanced crew. Dave the Jew owned his own handgun, but refused to part with it, which made me very jealous. We would engage larger gangs in combat with our World War One issue Australian Army bayonets, and we were undefeated.

Terry was bigger than me, and I wasn't small. Cowboy Johnny was a few years older than me, and a bit punchy. He wasn't a big thinker, but loyal.

Dave the Jew and I nearly fell out – it could have come to bloodshed and death – after Reggie the carpet snake bit him on the hand and he cut Reggie and Ronny both up with a meat axe.

Dave was sentenced to punishment. He had to eat a full packet of lit smokes one after the other, swallow them down with a bottle of ouzo then receive a sound beating. It was either that or a shot in both legs. Dave ate the cigarettes – all lit – then polished off the ouzo to kill the pain of the coming beating. We broke his face up well. In fact, he lost his front teeth. All was forgiven.

The Surrey Road gang didn't muck around. Cowboy Johnny wouldn't eat the smokes or drink the ouzo or take his beating so Dave shot him in both legs with a sawn-off .22. We dug the slugs out with a potato knife. Johnny then went to hospital. No slugs, no police.

Terry the Tank refused his punishment once and the three of us attacked him. Had Terry carried on and entered the criminal world full on, he would have been a force to be reckoned with. Physically, he was as strong as 10 men. however, we got him in the end. Dave was mad keen on shooting him in the legs, but Terry agreed on the standard pack of lit smokes, ouzo and a sound flogging.

A crew can't expect to dish it out if it can't take it as well, and we were a top crew. Violence and street combat was our religion. I was the general, and I ruled with an iron fist. Great days.

My 19th birthday party was going to be a big event in my life. To be honest I never had a proper birthday party. Seventh Day Adventist birthday parties for children in the Read home ended up as prayer meetings. So by the time I was turning 19 and not living at home I wanted a real one to make up for all the other years.

I set about getting ready for the big day. I had a one-bedroom flat in Williams Road, South Yarra. I emptied most of the furniture out. Then I rang the Thomastown Boys via 'Satchmo' and the Croydon Boys via 'Bernie'. I notified 'Terry the Tank' and his mates, 'Mad Charlie' and his crew, Horatio Morris and his old South and Port Melbourne mates, and Vincent Villeroy and his friends. I told them all to bring the biggest sluts they could lay their hands on. But I didn't tell any of the crews I'd invited that other crews were coming.

The big night had come. All was set. I had spent several hundred dollars on grog and the bath tub was full of ice. I put Cowboy Johnny Harris up on the roof of the flats next door with a walkie talkie and a 30–30 lever-action hunting rifle so he could let rip if any gatecrashers dared to pull up outside. No one came.

Only my dear old dad, 'Satchmo', a few of the Thomastown

boys and Robyn the policeman's daughter.

It turned out that bloody 'Terry the Tank' had rung around and every crew in Melbourne knew the other crews were coming. It was decided behind my back that my 19th would be a bloodbath. I've never tried to toss a party since.

Our gang kept a supply of weapons hidden in the toilets of the South Yarra Arms, the Morning Star hotel and later the Bush Inn hotel. We stashed one sawn-off shotgun, one tomahawk, one meat cleaver and one iron bar in each pub – an idea I got from what the Kray brothers did in London. We also had a very high-powered cattle prod stolen from the Newmarket cattle yards. When we got hold of the leadership of rival gangs, one blast of the cattle prod on the lower guts and their bowels dropped out – shit everywhere.

The Surrey Road gang was feared. We had blues with the Richmond boys regularly, but as there weren't many of us, we would go to the home address of our enemy and get him as he walked out, at his own front door. These are the same tactics used by the IRA. We once bashed a rival gang leader as he left the cemetery after his mother's funeral. Another time we broke the legs of the brother of an enemy – then caught the one we wanted in the waiting room of the Alfred Hospital. It was another IRA trick learnt from my reading of military history.

Terry the Tank is now a well-to-do honest member of the community with a wife and children. Cowboy Johnny is dead. Dave the Jew is living in South Yarra in relaxed comfort with his trust fund. And I'm where I am. That's the Surrey Road gang now ... a memory of my teenage years.

Chapter 3

Family and Friends

'Dad saved me a lot of bother ... and Brian Kane an early funeral.'

My dear old dad, Keith Alfred Read, served in the Australian Army for 24 years, the merchant navy for two years, and was a professional welterweight boxer for a while. As a result of his time in the ring he became friends and remained friends with the great Eddy Miller until Miller's death in the late 1960s.

During the 1939–45 war Dad served on the island of New Britain, then he went to Indonesia, Rabaul and other islands then to Japan, where he saw Hiroshima first hand.

Later, he joined the merchant navy for two years, then rejoined the army and served in the K Force in Korea.

On leaving the army the second time he worked for Apps funeral directors. Apps had the Government contract picking up all the homicide and suicide jobs.

My dad is well known to all the crims who know me. He has withstood gossip and slander in the streets where he's lived and countless death threats, all because of me. The stress and strain of my 20-odd years of police, prison and criminal trouble have taken their toll on Dad. However, he has stood with me rock solid and loyal through thick and thin. He would stand in front of me and take the bullet meant for me if he could. His love and loyalty is without question. What else can I say?

All my life Dad has slept with a gun beside his bed. And after his divorce from my mother he took to sleeping with a fully-loaded pump-action alongside him in the double bed, barrel pointing down towards his feet. But I got him out of that. It now goes under or alongside the bed on the floor. Getting up at night to go to the toilet, with my old dad and his trusty pump-action in the next room, meant yelling out: 'Going to the toilet, Dad,' so he knew who was walking around.

'Right, boy,' he would yell back. One thing, with the old soldier in the next room, armed up, I slept well.

Once, when he was young, Dad got the idea that the next-door neighbours were mistreating their family pet. Every time he looked over the fence the animal seemed to be getting thinner and thinner.

He complained to the neighbours, and said he hated cruelty to animals. Every time he asked them if they were feeding the dog, they swore they were. But it seemed skinnier than ever, and one day Dad could take no more. He jumped the fence, threatened the neighbour with a beating, then took the dog and drowned it to put it out of its misery.

It was the first time he had seen a greyhound.

Old time gunman Horatio Morris introduced me to an old Melbourne bookmaker we'll call Bert, a dark horse, behind-the-scenes man and quite a nice chap. And there was another fellow, a bookie called Pat. I met Pat years later in South Yarra in 1977. He was very close to Brian Kane. On the night in question Kane had pulled up outside an address in Rockley Road, South Yarra, to speak to a chap who had been roughing up Pat's lady friend. The address was right next to where my dad and I lived.

I grabbed Dad's pump-action shotgun – the old Bentley – loaded it with heavy shot and ran down and bailed Kane up. Having met him at the Morning Star Hotel in Prahran a month or so before in the company of police regarding a matter concerning Billy Longley, I was convinced he was in Rockley Road to kill me, and I had the barrel of the gun in his mouth.

My dad rushed out and calmed things down, allowing poor Brian to explain that he was on a mission of mercy regarding Pat's lady friend being belted by the chap in the address near us in Rockley Road. Whereupon, we all went in and spoke to the offender in question.

It was a close call. Dad saved me a lot of bother ... and Brian Kane an early funeral.

Margaret is the only real girlfriend I've ever had. She has stuck by me with love, loyalty and devotion since 1983. Don't ask me why, as I can't understand it myself.

Once, she was questioned by the homicide squad over me for five hours – and stuck rock solid. She was questioned by the Internal Security Unit three times running for hours at a time over me – and remained rock solid. She has withstood death threats too many times to count – over me. She sat through my murder trial. She has never failed me, let me down or betrayed me. She's got more heart, guts and dash than any man I've known.

I cannot explain how I really feel about this woman. I'm not a great romantic or a playboy. I'm not the hearts and flowers sort of man – and until Margaret I strongly believed that love of a romantic nature was never to find me. I was a lone wolf all my life until I met Margaret. To say that I love her seems a feeble way to describe my feelings. I owe this lady more than I could ever pay in 100 lifetimes. If I could put my finger on one reason for why I am really walking away from it all, Margaret would be the reason.

But a love affair with a crim with a price on his head is not all hearts and flowers, sometimes it's more like a war movie than a romance. Being covered in tattoos and hated by half the underworld has its drawbacks. Like when you want to go swimming, for instance.

Margaret and I used to love going to the beach – but we

had to pick nice out-of-the-way spots, as I am covered neck to ankle in tatts. And then there's the matter of security, which is why we had to take along quite a bit of hardware.

That consisted of a .25 calibre automatic handgun in Margaret's beach bag – along with a .32 calibre five-shot revolver, a .32 calibre automatic pistol, a .410 sawn-off shotgun, a .357 magnum revolver, a .44 magnum revolver, a .38 automatic pistol – and a .22 calibre 30-shot fully automatic cut-down machine gun fitted with a silencer.

That's eight firearms. I used to carry all I could with me, so 'beach time' was 'paranoid time'. I used to have a small eskie that floated on the water. I'd pop some ice and beer cans in it along with the cut down machine gun and take it out with me and swim and dive around near it.

I took no chances at all. Margaret had been taught to use the .25 automatic pistol. God, she looked great in her teeny weeny bikini. I loved taking her to the beach. However, if anyone else came to the beach I'd swim back and get ready for battle. Beach time could have turned into a nightmare, and I wanted to make sure no one was going to gun me down without a fighting chance.

If something had happened, I had full faith that Margaret would have blown them to hell. Like all Maltese women, she has a terrible temper. The first reaction of the Maltese female when angered is to head straight into the kitchen to the knife drawer. Once I had to run out the front door into the street with dear little Margaret in hot pursuit, carving knife in her hand and screaming at me.

I used to have to hide my guns after she picked up my .32 revolver and tried to pull the trigger on me. However, it was a stiff trigger and she couldn't make it work, thank God. Throwing heavy objects at me was another favourite. Mind you, I was always in the wrong, and no doubt needed telling off. But her temper was quite frightening. Once, while Margaret was driving me down Sydney Road, Brunswick in thick traffic, with me carrying several guns and a bag full of assorted other guns and ammo, we had an argument. She stopped the car in the middle of the traffic, got out, took the keys and stormed off down the street – leaving me sitting there, paranoid, expecting to be arrested any moment, and with other cars blowing their horns at me. Luckily, she took pity on me and came back. I've always found it wise never to anger little Margaret too much.

Her bad temper – and blood loyalty – were part of the reasons I love her so much. That and her teeny weeny bikini.

Two more friends I have to mention are 'Mad Micky' and his wife Lynn. They have shown me great kindness and friendship. When I got out of jail in November 1986, and went to Tassie to see my old dad, Lynn took me to the Launceston casino.

It was the first time I'd ever been into a real live legal gambling place. She showed me how to play roulette and I gave her the dough and she played for me. I was shocked to see her winning. We had a great time. I kept going back to the casino day after day – and winning a few hundred each day. I thought I must have had some magic touch, so I took my dad with me to show him what a great roulette player I was – and blew $2,000 in front of him. He stood there, shaking his head and looking at me as if I was a complete idiot. And I felt a complete idiot. That will teach me for showing off.

Mick is a great bloke – and also a friend of Craig 'Slim' Minogue's, and still keeps in touch with him today by post. A loyal chap, our Micky. He is nicknamed the 'Man John West Rejected' after getting arrested in Launceston for hijacking a truckload of frozen prawns. There was big money involved – but the comedy of being arrested over a lorryload of prawns is something he may never live down.

Once we brought Micky over to Melbourne for a bit of nightclub life – me and Amos Atkinson and Mad Charlie and a few of the boys. We had plans to take Micky and do all the clubs. But at the first hint of bloodshed Charlie stayed at home. Charlie is more a telephone gangster – lying under his doona in his big double bed making phone calls. And Amos bailed out as well, after meeting Mad Micky. So it was me and Micky and a nutcase crew of boys from the western suburbs.

We all had guns as normal. However, when we offered Micky a nice little .32 calibre revolver for the night out he said no. Off we went – to the Chevron first, then Bojangles.

Back in 1987 Bojangles was the biggest bloodhouse in Melbourne. We all knew there would be trouble on the night, but thought we wouldn't tell Micky.

As we expected, there was a large crew of Italian gents at Bojangles who had let it be known they would deal with me when they saw me next.

A .44 magnum can be a great weapon when used to pistol whip. At first when the two teams met there was a Mexican standoff – until I got proceedings under way with a sneaky pistol whip across the head of the leader of the other crew. Guns were produced all round. I rested the magnum on the shoulder of one of our crew, another Tasmanian named Andrew, and pulled the hammer back.

That was it. All guns out on both sides in a crowded nightclub, and everyone set to shoot each other. Poor Mick, being empty-handed, felt awful. He was standing there like a Chicago gangster with his hand in his coat pocket pretending he had a gun. We backed out of the nightclub, guns in hand, with poor Micky in front, using him as a shield. He still had his hand in his coat pocket with his finger pointing out.

The funny part was, we were told later, the other crew was worried about Mad Micky. We couldn't see it, but his eyes were blazing and he had a crazy face on – and they all thought he had a gun in his pocket. The redheaded guy in the long overcoat and mad look on his face had them bluffed.

Poor Micky. Invited out for a night on the town, then used as a cover to back out of a Mexican standoff in a nightclub. He didn't have much luck that night. He picked up a great-looking blonde at the Chevron ... only to learn 'she' was a drag queen. But his sense of humour didn't leave him. 'Bugger Melbourne,' said Micky. 'I'm going back to Tassie.'

When I see Mick again I suspect I will be the victim of some foul practical trick to repay me for the Bojangles débâcle.

Chapter 4

Dave the Jew

'Forgiveness and funerals go hand in hand, and the only time to forgive an enemy is after you have seen him die.' – The Jew

I can't give Dave the Jew's last name, but I can give you a short profile of him. He has been my close friend since I was 15 years old, and he is, to say the least, a very odd fellow. Very strange, indeed. But then, you'd expect a bloke with no ears to have strange friends, wouldn't you?

Dave is an occasional criminal and part-time gunman – but without a criminal record. He has never had his prints taken and the police don't even know he exists, but he has mixed with and done work for some big-time criminals, including a few of your so-called Mr Bigs. Not all the dangerous men get talked about in the newspapers or end up in court rooms or prison cells.

Dave is sometimes called 'Meyer Blue Eyes' because of his vivid blue eyes. He has an uncle in America called 'Al Malnik', a Jewish money man who was groomed by the late American Jewish financial underworld figure

Meyer Lansky. I know it all sounds totally unbelievable – but the FBI could tell you who 'Al Malnik' is.

Dave the Jew is also close to Abe Saffron's family, Abe being some sort of a Dutch uncle of Dave's. His father was a well-known Melbourne restaurant owner, and another relative is a clothing manufacturer in Melbourne. His mother died recently; he was born and bred in South Yarra, educated at Wesley College, is a non-smoker and non-drinker, and can't drive a car – although he sometimes insists on doing so.

Dave has been a close personal friend of a top IRA man for years, and spent six months in Ireland in 1975 or 1976. The Jew is a great man for international politics. He has collected $15,000 for the Sinn Fein but he has donated half of it to the Orange Lodge here in Melbourne. Talk about having a foot in either camp. The Jew says he has mates in both camps, so it is only fair. Apart from that, he has always liked having a bit each way.

He spent about nine months in the Israeli Army in 1980–1981, then deserted. He can never return to Israel again – they would shoot him. He was locked up in a fort in the Philippines, but escaped and returned to Australia.

He has undergone treatment for a mental condition – paranoia – and sometimes believes he is the living, breathing spirit or reincarnation of the late American-Jewish gangster Benny 'Bugsy' Siegel.

Dave is a lot of things. He is as mad as a hatter, as shifty as a shithouse rat, as smart as a whip and as dangerous as a black snake on a dark night. And a true and loyal friend, which is why I cannot betray his name.

Several unsolved murders can be put down to Dave the Jew.

One of the strangest things about Dave, as the son of strict Jewish parents, was his constant reading of Adolf Hitler's *Mein Kampf*. I asked him one day why he read such a book and he looked at me and replied quietly: 'Know thy enemy.'

I have always remembered that, and I have used that tactic ever since. For example, how do you locate an enemy if you don't know where he is living or if he is in hiding? Locate his mum and dad's address. The one day of the year when you can bet that your enemy or target will be at a certain address is Christmas Day at his mum's place. Most people go to Mum's on Christmas Day ... unless your name is Chopper Read, in which case you go and have a counter lunch. Even Christmas Day would not induce me to eat steamed chicken.

Another fact is that most men can be located either at a funeral or in a hospital waiting room – the trick being to get them to those two spots. And all ethnic people love their mothers. Once you have explained a matter to 'Mummy' she will speak to her son for you. Bingo.

Know thy enemy. Basic Black and Tan logic and tactics. The Black and Tans being the feared paramilitary unit used by the British Army against the IRA in the early part of this century. I won't go into Black and Tan methods of carrying out interrogations. Suffice to say that I said to (Lynas Patrick)

Driscoll once that I considered the removal of toes to be rather humane by comparison.

Speaking of which, Dave the Jew rang me one day in 1977 and asked could I come to an address in Port Melbourne. I took a taxi from Rockley Road, South Yarra, armed to the teeth and carrying a small bag containing a hand–held gas bottle and blowtorch.

The game was afoot, if you get my meaning. Dave the Jew was the best headhunter and catcher I'd ever known. He'd been drinking with a crew of Irish seamen on the advice of Vincent Villeroy, the old Irish boxer, soldier and standover man we knew. One of these seamen – we'll call him Sweeney – was working on a bodgie ticket and papers. He was bringing smack into Melbourne. Neither Dave nor I had the slightest interest in smack, but on Vincent's advice we watched and waited, ready to pounce, until cash changed hands.

Dave had lain under a house in Port Melbourne with a sleeping bag, pillow, and cans of lemonade and baked beans from Friday until Saturday night. It was about 2 a.m. on the Sunday morning when, at last, Sweeney staggered up the driveway to visit his old mother, drunk as a lord.

'Bloody mothers,' said Dave. 'They will be the death of us all.' Ha ha. Dave often made mother jokes. Poor old Sweeney didn't even get to wake Mum up. Dave had got him.

An iron bar over a drunk's head is pretty useless, but across the back of the neck not too hard, it puts a drunk to sleep.

You have to know what you're doing, or you can shatter the central nervous system. But the Jew was an old hand at this technique. In no time Sweeney was asleep in the boot of the car.

We drove a short distance to a hotel where Vincent Villeroy said we could use the cellar without making any noise.

There I was, Dr Chopper with his medical bag, doing a night call at this pub in Port Melbourne. Vincent let me in, and stayed in the back bar drinking with the publican, pretending to have no idea whatsoever that 'torture most foul' was to take place in the keg cellar.

I went down and shut the trap behind me. There was Dave the Jew trying to revive a sleeping Sweeney, to no avail. 'Take his shoes and socks off,' I said. 'This will liven him up.' I pulled the gas bottle out, turned it on and lit her up, adjusting the flame to a good yellow, not a fine blue. I wanted to produce pain, not cut his feet off. I put the flame to the sole of the bare foot. Dave held it up for me. Within a matter of 20 seconds the sole was bubbling, snap–crackle–pop, a burning mess. Flesh burns because of the fat content.

The smell was shocking. The fumes had reached the nostrils of Vincent and the publican. The trap door went up. It was the bloody publican's wife. 'Jesus Christ!' she screamed. We dropped the foot and ran up the stairs. It was havoc.

The publican was out cold. Vincent had knocked him out. The publican's wife was screaming. Her three kiddies in their night clothes were standing in the stairway asking what the matter was. Twenty years jail flashed through my mind. Dave had his gun out and wanted to kill every living human being in the pub. This was toe-cutter comedy at its most insane. To top it off we could still smell the fumes of Sweeney's bloody foot. It was alight, smoking and smelling terrible.

'Aaah!' screamed the publican's wife. She grabbed a fire extinguisher, ran down the cellar stairs and put the foot out. Dave turned to old Vincent, yelling, 'You stupid punchy Irish bastard! I thought you said the bloody pub was empty!'

'No problem,' said Vincent. 'They won't tell.'

'Won't tell,' yelled Dave. 'I'm killing them anyway!'

This was a tricky one. We had seen Dave the Jew like this before, his blue eyes ablaze, gun in hand. Too much *Mein Kampf*, if you ask me.

It was obvious the general had to take control before Dave shot the household, including myself and Vincent.

'OK,' I said to Dave. 'They are off.

Dave relaxed. 'Vinnie,' I said to Vincent, 'give Dave a hand.' I winked as I said it, and as Dave looked away the old ex-heavyweight pug knocked the Jew out.

'Right, cuff him and put him in the boot,' I said.

By this time the publican had woken up. 'Right,' I said. 'We're out of here. Give us a hand with the stiff in the cellar.' Me and the publican carried Sweeney out to the car and laid him in the back seat. Vinnie was still trying to secure the boot so Dave couldn't escape. Me, Vinnie and the publican went back in. The kids were put to bed quickly. We all had a stiff whisky. The pub still stank of burnt flesh. I promised the publican and his wife two grand each for compo, and that Vinnie would deliver it. No problem, said the publican and his wife. Thank you for that.

Back in the car we had a kicking and screaming Dave in the boot. 'Shut up!' I yelled as we drove along. 'Or I'll pump a few through the back seat.' Dave shut up. I said to Vinnie: 'When's this bastard's ship leave?'

He looked at his watch and said, 'In about half an hour.'

I said: 'Right, get him back on the ship. Give me the Jew's gun and cuff keys and let me out now.' Vincent pulled up. I opened the boot and pulled Dave out. He was angry but in control. I undid his cuffs, tossed the cuffs and keys in the boot and said to Vincent: 'This is your fuck-up. You fix it.'

He said: 'I'm sorry, Chopper. I'm sorry.'

I said: 'Piss off, now. Go.'

Dave and I walked in the cold night air, calming down. 'We would be better off with a cut lunch and a nine to five,' said Dave.

We both laughed. We had been through a lot, the mad Jew and I, and we loved each other like brothers. We saw a taxi and hailed it, and went back to Dave's home in South Yarra. We woke his mum and had a nice sit-down dinner.

Dave's mum said: 'You both smell like burnt hair.' His dad came down – and knew the smell after one sniff.

'I haven't smelt that smell since 1943' he said.

'It's not what you think, father' Dave said.

'Don't tell me,' said Dave's dad. 'You smell like a Belsen barbecue. I'm going back to bed.'

As it turned out, Vincent did fix it. Sweeney slept unconscious through the whole thing and is now living in Spain.

I can tell a lot of stories about Dave.

Once he was contracted to do a hit on a major underworld figure — a Sydney identity visiting Melbourne for the November racing calendar. Dave the Jew was armed with a Colt Armalite AR-15 Sporter, which loads with a 5.56mm NATO round. The gun was fitted with a 'scope, and he had a 30-round clip.

The 'victim' was staying with friends in a house in the eastern suburbs. There had been some planning and expense put in beforehand. A flat had been rented across the road under a bodgie name eight weeks before the Sydneysider's November visit. It was a balcony flat on the second floor. The front window of the flat was no use because there were trees in the way, so the shot had to be from the side balcony. On the day, Dave took up his position and watched as the target and his wife and son walked towards a Ford LTD which was waiting for them.

Dave suddenly decided to climb over the balcony rail and sit with one leg each side of the rail to get a better aim. It was a fairly easy 180-yards shot. He leaned out to the side a bit, taking perfect aim for the classic heart shot. But just as he was about to squeeze the trigger he slipped and fell off his perch.

It was two storeys from the balcony to the rock and cactus garden below, and Dave's screams of pain brought the 'victim' and his son running across the street to see what was wrong. They found Dave the Jew in great pain with a broken arm, and bruised and bleeding. By chance the rifle had landed on the other side of the fence out of sight. The Sydney man and his wife and son and a friend drove the Jew to hospital. Later Dave sent a thank you card to the Sydney chap.

It is an embarrassing true story, going to prove that the best of us can go arse over elbow. I thought being driven to hospital by the unsuspecting 'murder victim' was a touch of Hitchcock. They simply thought the poor fellow had fallen from the balcony.

There's a postscript to that story. The chap who did all the beforehand planning and paid Dave $20,000 cash up front to do the hit was later shot dead himself ... not long after he demanded his money back and threatened the Jew's life. Ha ha.

In early 1987, in Collingwood, I had four shots fired at me from a moving car. I made phone calls to various people and tried to have the offenders identified and located. I received information that it might be an Italian crew from Carlton. I rang Dave the Jew and demanded he case all the clubs in Carlton.

The Jew obtained a Salvation Army uniform and hat and

collection tin – and a dozen copies of the *War Cry* – and he did Lygon Street. He noted that they are a 'bloody good-hearted lot' in Lygon Street: he made some $200-odd dollars, most of it from the clubs. However, an observant eye would have picked one flaw in the Jew's cunning covert operation. The Salvos don't collect money at two o'clock in the morning.

He reported back on key figures, car rego numbers, club telephone numbers, where different people parked their cars, approximate nightly cash turnover – and the number of fire extinguishers, a key factor. He reported access to rear exits and the width of entrance stairs.

I was considering a little IRA tactic called 'petrol and plenty of it.' However, I was approached by certain police who swore to me that this crew was not guilty. I was of two minds about believing this or not. Dave, however, felt a fire was a wonderful idea, and that guilt could be determined after the event. The fact that the police knew about the shots fired at me, and police interest in my feelings re Lygon Street, and the fact guilt had never been proven, led me to cancel 'Operation Wog Fry.'

It was a case where a peace meeting between my good self and the police stopped a war. We were going to turn part of Lygon Street into an inferno. I think Dave was a little disappointed we didn't go ahead with the barbecue.

Dion was an Irishman – a seaman who went to Melbourne at

least once a year. I met him through Dave the Jew. Dion now lives in South Africa and won't be returning, so it's OK to tell this story.

In 1977 an argument broke out between Dion and Dave the Jew. Dave rang me and wanted me to come to his home in South Yarra. When I got there I found a badly-wounded Dion. Dave had shot him three times in the back, once in the chest, once in the buttocks, and once in the upper left leg. Dave had used a .32 calibre revolver.

Dion could not be taken to hospital, and he was lying on Dave's mother's kitchen table. He had to be moved and the kitchen cleaned before Dave's mum and dad got home.

We moved him to a mate's house, then got together a razor blade, a sharp knife, a bottle of peroxide, penicillin powder and a bottle of antibiotics. Then we sent our other mate out to get two grams of heroin and a needle.

We gave Dion a small hit of heroin to kill the pain, then I king hit him twice on the jaw, as he lay naked on the bathroom floor, to knock him out cold. Then we cut and dug the slugs out. Every time he woke up I smashed him again to put him out. After the operation I gave him another shot of heroin. He was in noddy land.

We cleaned all the wounds with peroxide, dusted them all heavily with penicillin powder and bandaged and plastered the wounds and made him swallow four antibiotics. He slept and slept. When he woke up we gave him antibiotics and vitamin B, vitamin E and vitamin C. If he died we'd bury him. I left. Dave nursed him for ten days – changing his dressings, pumping antibiotics and vitamins into him, keeping him warm.

Dion lived. He left and went to Ireland. He later went to South Africa. Doctor Chopper rides again.

Dave has always been a deep thinker. He said, 'Forgiveness and funerals go hand in hand and the only time to forgive an enemy is after you have seen him die.'

He loves to quote the Irish author Brendan Behan who said, 'The Irish and the Jews have a psychosis.'

He also quoted him as saying, 'A general bit of shooting makes you forget your troubles and takes the mind off the cost of living.' I have a feeling he may be planning a little bit of a comedy of his own in the future because he has quoted Israeli General Moshe Dayan as saying during the six day war, 'If we lose this war I'll start another one in my wife's name.'

I think that might mean he has plans to reopen an old war and I think I know who with. The Jew hates unfinished business.

I'll miss the Jew. I've told him he can come to Tassie for a visit. I'll take him fishing, a stick of 'gellie' in the river and bang, we'll be knee deep in trout. I've never had the patience for rod and reel.

THE JEW

He wants no glory, he wants no fame,
Very few men have heard his name.
But as a hunter, he's the best I know
Non-stop dash, non-stop go,
He sets to work, without a care,
The smell of burning flesh in the air,
He loves to hunt the big deal prankster,
The nightclub flashy gangster,
He plants them in the ground,
Never to be seen,
Safe and sound,
And before they die, they sometimes ask,
Please tell me who are you,
And with a toothless grin, he looks down and says,
Just call me Dave the Jew.

Chapter 5

Cowboy Johnny

'Another kick and I'd have been dead ... Johnny charged in, bayonet in hand, and gave his life to save mine.'

COWBOY Johnny Harris was the bastard son of a well-known Prahran prostitute. He used to stand watch in laneways in Prahran, Windsor and St Kilda when he was 10 years old, looking out for police while his mum took care of customers in the laneway.

He could neither read nor write. I met him when I was about 15 and he was 20 or so, but he was quite childlike in the mind and I never felt younger than him. He was five foot nine inches tall, about eleven stone seven, had a slightly hunched back, a 19-inch neck, cauliflower ears and battered facial features. He was an evil-looking bloke.

The Cowboy was born in a brothel in Port Melbourne in the late 1940s. No doctor was called, no birth certificate issued. He was never christened or baptised. He never knew his father – and neither did his mother. 'Harris' was just a name his mother told him to use. His mum died in a mental hospital in the late 1960s – suicide. He had no living relatives at the time of his death. Prahran was full of Johnny's 'uncles' – in other words, blokes who knew his mother.

He spent his first few years in the brothel, was tormented and teased at school because he was a bastard, and left when he was 10 years old. He learned to fight early, and it became about the only thing he could do better than most.

When I was only 16 or 17, Johnny and I would enter the illegal bare-knuckle fights. You could earn $100 if you won and $50 if you lost – but you also made money on the tips and side bets. It was a bloodbath. For little or no money, you'd get your head beaten in. Old men betting on young boys to punch themselves half to death for chicken feed.

As a kid, Johnny also boxed in Sharman's tent show. He boxed in the tent every year at the Royal Melbourne Show under the name 'Cowboy Johnny'.

The tent fighters were a violent and bloody group. I remember once we were walking up Toorak Road in South Yarra, and a gentleman hopped out of a Rolls Royce motor car, went around to the footpath side to let out a lovely young woman, all dressed nice to step into a fine South Yarra restaurant. As we passed them the Cowboy stepped in and crashed the gent with a left hook to the point of the jaw. He fell and didn't get up. I kept walking – faster, I might add. When Johnny caught up we turned a corner and both ran. When we stopped I said: 'For God's sake, Johnny. What was that all about?'

He said to me: 'I had my last dinner yesterday, and it doesn't look as if I'll be getting another one until tomorrow, and them bastards are going to spend a week's pay on a feed.'

I looked at Johnny, then I took him home and my dad cooked him a slap-up dinner. After that Cowboy Johnny Harris would have killed any man who bad-mouthed my old dad. Dad gave him good, clean secondhand clothes and footwear – and bought him his first toothbrush. My father's kindness to the Cowboy was remembered later.

In December 1972, my father, aged 47, and at five foot ten and 15 stone, could still put his punches together quite nicely, and he found himself in a fist fight with a larger man half his age in Williams Road, South Yarra. The other fellow also used a knuckle duster. I was in Pentridge at the time doing three months for assaulting three police. My father won the fight in nice style – but suffered some cutting about because of the knuckle duster. Johnny found out, and hunted the other chap down for about three weeks, cornered him in a hotel lounge bar in Prahran and with no howdy-dos stepped in and with six to ten punches shattered the other chap's jaw, cheekbones and nose. Then he walked up to the bar, picked up a beer glass, broke it and delivered the 'coup de grace' – leaving the other chap with part of his chin and lip hanging off. He then left the pub without a word.

My dad was the father Cowboy never had, and the Cowboy

loved him dearly.

I don't wish to go into the details of Cowboy's death, as it is still upsetting. It happened when Johnny took on an army in a street battle in Richmond. I was being kicked to death – another good kick and I'd have been dead. Johnny charged in, army bayonet in hand, and gave his life to save mine.

The truth about the Cowboy was that he had punched and kicked three men to death during the late 1960s and early 1970s. He was no angel during the sharpie street battles of those days. There was a code in those days, not only with myself; you didn't leave a fallen mate in the street to die like a dog, and no one wanted any police involvement.

A lot of things got handled privately and the details are hard to explain. Many people who are still about would be outraged if I told the whole story and if they thought I had given up all the details. The bloke died saving my life. I held him in my arms as he bled to death from a broken bottle in the neck.

The Jew got there late. He sat with me, and we cried while Johnny died. I am not going any further about it; I will have to leave it at that.

If Dave the Jew and I had not paid for the cremation service Johnny would have been buried a nameless unknown vagrant in a pauper's grave. How we got him cremated is our business. His life was a tragedy. His happiest days were with the Surrey Road Gang. Johnny's goodbye was our personal concern. He was our brother and our comrade. Sending him off was for us alone.

Johnny always said he wanted to be burnt up when he died, and his ashes spread on the water – but not the sea, because he didn't want the fishes to eat his remains. He once told us where he wanted his ashes put. And that's what he got.

On the day of his funeral Dave and I met at the Morning Star Hotel. Dave carried a bag with an urn containing the mortal remains. He also carried in the bag a cut-down .22 calibre rifle with a special 30-shot clip. I carried a battery-operated cassette player with the Cowboy's favourite song on the tape – an old 1950s rock 'n' roll song, 'Sea of Heartbreak'. We drank at the Morning Star until closing time. Dave and I were quite tearful by then. We walked quietly along drinking from a bottle of good Irish whiskey until we got to the Prahran Swimming Pool and Baths on Malvern Road, across the road from the Prahran commission flats.

We broke the lock and went in. The night lights were on. We stood at the side of the pool and put the cassette player on and turned it up loud, and 'Sea of Heartbreak' rang out loud. Dave handed me the urn and I removed the lid, lifted it up high and and said: 'Goodbye, Cowboy. We love you, brother.' Then I tipped the ashes into the water while Dave fired off 21 shots in the air with the cut-down .22.

I had tears running down my face. So did Dave. We didn't care if anyone came along. We stood until 'Sea of Heartbreak' ended. Then we turned and walked away.

When next you use the Prahran swimming pool, spare a thought for Cowboy Johnny.

Three of the main offenders who took part in nearly killing me and killing the Cowboy are now dead themselves. 'Revenge is a dish best eaten cold.'

Terry the Tank had left the Surrey Road gang and I was getting around with Mad Charlie. However, the offenders in the Richmond kicking matter had a Jewish problem which they didn't realise. Dave the Jew took care of the three ringleaders over a period of years.

I am sorry to say I was in jail for all three 'goodbyes' – but nobody escapes the Jew. He watched and waited, slept under houses, stood in the rain and cold for hours and travelled by foot for days. He didn't rest until Johnny had been revenged. The Jew felt that because he had been late arriving to the Richmond blue that my near-death and Johnny's death fell on his shoulders – and that it was his debt of honour to get even.

The mind boggles at how those three died, as all three simply didn't come home. One by one, they vanished. But if you can envisage a *Mein Kampf*-reading Jew being treated for a mental condition you might imagine what happened.

We were a hard crew, and followed violent rules. Loyalty without question and revenge or death was the creed we agreed upon. The Surrey Road gang made the mafia look like poofs.

It is no secret that from time to time in jail over the years I have not enjoyed the best of mental health.

There was a high-pressure point in late 1983 after I was released from Jika. As I walked from Jika up to the mainstream of Pentridge, I was convinced I was walking into a bloodbath. Then a familiar voice spoke to me.

I looked over my shoulder and there was Cowboy Johnny Harris walking behind me. I was told by prisoners and prison staff that for a few days my face and eyes had a crazy look. I spent two days talking to a dead man. In my mind I was convinced he was walking with me. I was in a highly dangerous state of mind.

THE COWBOY

His friendship I can't forget, I'll remember him till I die,
And sometimes in the dead of night I think of him and cry.
He fought his way into my heart, head butt, fist and tooth,
His shadow always with me, a memory from my youth,
No one's guts were stronger, no one's heart more true,
And no one loved him more than me and Dave the Jew,
He gave his life that I should live,
And the dogs who killed him we don't forgive,
That's a tale the Jew won't tell,
But all of them now rest in Hell,
The man without a name, a father or a mother,
Cowboy Johnny Harris, you're not forgotten, Brother.

Chapter 6

Mad Charlie

'Charlie studied Mafia crime books like a priest studied the Bible.'

'MAD Charlie' was a friend from my teenage days. He looked and sounded like a comic book gangster as a young man. He had dreams of greatness within the underworld. Once, in 1974, he went to America with his mum and dad, where he got to shake hands and say 'hello' to Carlo Gambino, the boss of bosses of the American Mafia. Carlo Gambino was head of the Gambino crime family, the largest of New York's five Mafia crime families.

Charlie was only 17 years old then, and returned with a heart full of dreams and a head full of big ideas. We saw the *Godfather* movie together. Charlie studied Mafia crime books like a priest studied the Bible. As a young up-and-coming criminal he had guts, brains and a small gang. Even as a teenager he was noted for his horrific violence in a street fight. He dressed expensively and had a style and class and flair that drew the attention of the main players in the criminal world.

I acted as Charlie's personal bodyguard along with 'Mad Archie', a streetfighter who had punched in the heads of such men as Brian Kane and others of that ilk. As a gang of young standover men in 1973–1974 we had no equals. I was an 18-stone giant with a total disregard for the so-called kingpins of the Melbourne underworld. I wanted to launch an all-out gang street war with the criminal world, and sit Mad Charlie on the throne. It sounded like a teenage criminal dream – but we had the guns and the wise advice of men like Horatio Morris directing me with tactics and targets.

Had Charlie given the go-ahead in 1974, I had a death list and enough M26 hand grenades to knock a giant hole in the Melbourne underworld – a hole big enough for us to walk through. But back then Mad Charlie didn't fully understand the power and total insanity of the men he had with him. By the time he found out, it was too late for Charlie. He had lost the energy that fuelled him.

Charlie got the nickname 'The Don' as the result of a raid on a St Kilda massage parlour in 1974. In Mad Archie's cherry red GT HO, armed with baseball bats, we cruised off to St Kilda. Charlie in the back seat with his always handy copy of Mario Puzo's book *The Godfather*. Charlie said in jest: 'Chopper, you can be Luca Brasi; Archie, you can be Paulie Gatto.' He made Garry the Greek his adviser. Then we asked who he was going to be, and he said: 'I'm the Don, of course'. So, in fits of laughter, off we went to St Kilda with Mad Archie at the wheel. He brought the big GT HO to a screaming halt across the footpath in front of the parlour in question; we ran out like screaming wild Indians and got to the front door ... but where was Mad Charlie?

We looked around and there was Charlie sitting in the back of the car, reading his beloved *Godfather* book. I went back and opened the door of the car. Charlie got out and said: 'That's right, Chopper: never forget the Don'.

'Never forget the Don!' indeed. Bloody Mad Charlie was sitting there waiting for me to open the door for him. To this day those close to Charlie still call him 'the Don'.

We didn't know it then, but that raid and others like it was the high point in Charlie's criminal career. Raiding the parlours in the cherry red GT HO started what the papers called the 1974 'parlour war' in the Prahran, Armadale, St Kilda, and Elsternwick areas.

However, five years jail saw Charlie bashed twice in fair fighting at the hands of Frankie Waghorn. Charlie's failure to revenge it saw him lose face in the criminal world. His failure to back me in the Overcoat Gang war in Pentridge meant that in the world of real blood and guts his name no longer counted. In 1987 I told Charlie I would back him in a war within the underworld that would have put him on top of the heap, but he had lost his guts for true violence, and he declined.

In late 1989, he was shot in the guts in front of his

$250,000 South Caulfield home. He's still alive, but his dreams of underworld glory never reached his teenage fantasies. All he has now are his mafia books and his collection of gangster videos.

But to the underworld kingpins who might laugh at Charlie now ... in 1974 one word from him could have seen them all dead, and changed the face of the underworld for ever. We had the death list, the guns and the insanity to carry it out.

Chapter 7

Ita Buttrose, Bloodshed and Me

'The drag queen had a body like Maggie Tabberer and a head like Henry Bolte, topped off with a big pair of silicone tits … I hit it over the head with a bucket and bit off its ear.'

Anyone who knows me well knows I have the words 'I LOVE ITA BUTTROSE' tattooed on my bum. The explanation for this is simple enough. All the boys in H Division loved Ita because the only magazines we were allowed there during the early and mid-1970s were the *Readers Digest* and *Women's Weekly*.

For a joke Jimmy Loughnan and I started the H Division branch of the Ita Buttrose fan club. Personally, I feel that if God had a mother she would look like Ita. How could any man not love Ita?

I haven't spoken much about real violence, so I will give a small true example of how my regard for Ita nearly got a bloke killed.

It was 1977, and I was in an inner-city pub when a well-known criminal and gunman made the mistake of bad-mouthing the sainted name of Ita, the woman of my dreams. I will not tell you this drunken lout's real name. I will simply call him 'One-eyed Pauly'. We fought tooth and nail, and this bloke could fight. To be honest, he could punch my head in – but for one thing. What I lack in the finer points of fisticuffs I make up for in violence. As far as I'm concerned the Marquess of Queensberry was a poof.

I got him with a series of head butts and elbow blows, a handful of hair and a knee to the face. When he went down I kicked him until he was out cold – and his face all smashed up. I made sure he lost an eye that day, which is how he got the nickname One-eyed Pauly. This was a dockies' pub and the onlookers were a pretty critical audience, so I had to make sure I left the right impression.

As I said when I finished my beer after the fight, I'd kill any man who spoke ill of Ita Buttrose.

You don't get a reputation like mine for being a nice guy.

In 1977 I had a bit of action to catch up on after getting out of jail after serving nearly three years for robbing massage parlours. I was out for five months before I walked into the County Court and kidnapped Judge Martin in January 26, 1978, which is another story.

In the five months I was out, I shot five men. I was charged and convicted for only one shooting – that of 'Johnny Corral' – a young criminal and knockabout not much older than myself. I got him in the left leg around the kneecap. Since then Johnny has carried a bad crippled leg. He has returned to prison several times, where my spies tell me news of his physical wellbeing.

I have always felt guilty over Johnny's gimpy leg. It happened because he was getting a bit lippy and got me on the wrong day. But if Johnny is reading this and remembers back, he must admit I did have the barrel at his head, then I reconsidered and dropped it to his leg. We were both young. Why he got loud-mouthed with a man carrying a shotgun is beyond me, but Johnny and his gimpy leg have played on my mind for years.

There was no hate or personal malice involved. It was just the way it went. I guess I'm trying to say I'm sorry about Johnny. If I could wave a magic wand and fix his gimpy leg, I would. The bloke stuck solid after I shot him and said nothing to the police. Sorry about that, Johnny.

In March 1975, in Pentridge's D Division in the billet's yard I was getting a haircut one day when I saw the strangest fight in my life. It was between 'Tiger Tommy Wells', an ex-boxer and former Australian titleholder of the 1960s, and a drag queen named Kelly.

Tiger Tommy was a tall, lanky, big-boned man with a lot of fistic skill. The drag queen was the roughest-looking piece of work God ever shovelled guts into – a body like Maggie Tabberer and a head like Henry Bolte, topped off with a big pair of silicone tits. 'She' was a sight to be seen.

The fight was fast and hectic. However, Tommy was a kind-hearted and gentle-natured chap with not a drop of violence in him, whereas Kelly the drag queen was as mad as a meat axe and about as dangerous.

I didn't fancy Tommy's chances. Sure enough, after five or so minutes of savage punching Tommy hit the deck. The drag queen then started to kick Tommy. Enough was enough. I stepped in, smashed the drag queen over the head with a mop bucket and bit its ear off.

'She' ran screaming and bleeding from the yard. I then helped Tommy up. I couldn't stand by and watch a good bloke like Tommy humiliated any further at the hands of such a creature.

I was sad to learn years later that Tiger Tommy hanged himself in the Ferntree Gully lockup. He was a gentleman and showed me great kindness. For a man like him to die in such a way in such a place was a tragedy.

Back in the days when I used to work out at Ambrose Palmer's gym I made the acquaintance of a former Australian heavyweight boxing champion who, for legal reasons and because he probably wouldn't thank me for mentioning him, I will not name.

However, in early 1973 I was having a drink in the Southern Cross Hotel in the city. I had to pop into the men's room and there I found the former champ engaged in fistic combat with a giant fellow – an American rather well known in Melbourne for his appearances on television's world championship wrestling, which was on every Sunday morning through the 1960s and 1970s. His name was 'Playboy Gary Hart'.

I didn't know what to do. The former Australian champ was punching – but to no avail. I went outside, walked to the bar, picked up a half-full jug of beer, tossed the beer out, went back into the men's room and smashed the big Yank over the skull. That slowed him down enough for the ex-champ to stiffen him with a very nice right uppercut. The big fellow was flat out on the floor.

I thought that was that. But then the ex-champ bent down and removed his Rolex watch, his rings, gold chains and wallet, and together we left the bar. As we got to the street I realised I was still holding half a broken beer jug by the handle, so I put it in the bin. The ex-champ put the rings, jewellery, watch and dough in his pocket. I said: 'You've got a watch. I want that one. Fair's fair.' So I got the Rolex.

About three weeks later, I was in Surfer's Paradise, enjoying the sun and surf and trying to find an opal dealer, massage-parlour owner, drug dealer and all round wealthy fellow called 'Chinese Charlie'.

It was hot and I was thirsty, so I walked into a lovely air-conditioned lounge bar for a cold beer. As I got inside and adjusted my eyes to the dimmer inside light I saw a big bloke at the bar who looked a bit too familiar. It was Playboy Gary Hart. He was standing at the bar looking at me, trying to remember where he knew me from. Beside him was a bald-headed giant I knew right away from the wrestling on TV and Saturday night at Festival Hall as 'Brute Bernard'.

I did a U-turn and walked back out. I couldn't get out of there fast enough. Gary Hart maybe, but I wouldn't fight old Brute Bernard unless I was carrying a chainsaw. Besides, I was still wearing the Playboy's gold Rolex.

'Bugger Chinese Charlie', I thought, and went back to Melbourne.

There's another yarn involving the Chinese, but this time one called Micky, who was from Sydney. As a favour, and for several thousand dollars, I met him because he had a problem to solve.

His niece had been raped and robbed and ripped off by her body-builder, karate-expert boyfriend, Steve the Greek, who had fled to Melbourne.

Steve was a NSW gangster. The shifty Chinese had tried to kill him in Sydney, but Steve the Greek bashed the attackers. He could fight like ten men, so I was asked to locate him, which was easy. He was a gambler, and it's not hard to find a Greek crook who plays cards in Melbourne, as Melbourne is a second Greece.

All I had to do was find him, grab him, hold him for the Chinese and call them when he was 'in custody'. To cut this story short, I did find him, I did render him unconscious and I took him to a house in Footscray and nailed his left hand to a large, heavy Franco Cozzo coffee table with a claw hammer and a roofing nail. Who says Franco Cozzo furniture is no good for anything?

One does not escape and run too far with one's hand nailed to such a large wooden coffee table. I rang the Chinese and they came and collected him ... and as far as I'm concerned that's the end of the story. The reason I'm being coy about it is that for all I know Steve the Greek may have ended up in 1,000 Chinese dim sims. None of my business.

For a short time in 1972 I boxed with Jimmy Sharman's boxing troupe in the sideshow tent fights. During the 1972 Royal Melbourne Show a right royal brawl broke out between myself and a well-known Melbourne street fighter, known to one and all as 'Stretch'. He beat me quite soundly. I was humbled and ashamed and left Sharman's and never boxed with gloves on again. 'Stretch' was a tall, thickset chap, bigger than myself – or he certainly seemed to be. I didn't know a lot about him, except that he had a huge reputation as a boxer and streetfighter, and had a highly popular following. He was also a bouncer in Prahran.

He was working at a dance at a ballroom in Greville Street at the time I located him. It was a cold, rainy Saturday night and big Stretch was standing in the doorway. As I walked towards him he nodded and said: 'How are you, young fella? No hard feelings?'

I said: 'Of course not. Even being beaten by you is an

honour, Stretch.' Then we shook hands. As I clasped his right hand with mine I rammed my left forefinger deep into his right eye socket, then headbutted him a vicious blow, and kneed him in the balls. He went down groaning.

I then finished him with a number of fast, heavy, vicious kicks to the head, face and throat. Stretch was down, out and lying on the footpath in the rain. Why? Because my smiling face when I approached him put him at ease. I maintained the big, wide, warm smile throughout. The whole thing took less than 60 seconds.

When it comes to violence, Chopper wrote the book.

I will tell the story of Turkish George, who was once a well-known, up and coming, long-haired, three-piece-suit-wearing heroin dealer and pimp in Fitzroy Street, St Kilda.

One day, I had popped in to the Prince of Wales Hotel for a counter lunch and a drink. I had just finished a lovely porterhouse steak, chips, eggs and mushrooms, all washed down with four or five pots of beer. I was standing in front of the pub, picking my teeth and enjoying the sunshine and watching the passing parade.

I saw a young girl, she looked about 13, wearing a short, white summer frock with white Roman sandals. She had lovely blonde hair and was about five foot. She would have looked very pretty if it wasn't for the fact she was sobbing, and had tears and a smattering of blood down her face.

I asked her what was the matter and she told me that

Turkish George had bashed her. I asked her why and she told me, this little schoolgirl, that she was using smack and doing dirty deeds at the weekend to pay for it. She still had some personal pride and wouldn't do some of the dirty deeds that Turkish George wanted her to do. She said she was only a part-time user and didn't have a habit.

She pointed out Turkish George, then I asked her whether she knew me. She said she didn't. I then asked her if she had heard of Chopper Read. She said she had heard the name in the street.

I said, 'I am Chopper Read ... and you are going to run on home and never show your face in St Kilda again.' She promised me she would clear out, and left.

I walked up the street a bit and saw Turkish George sitting in the passenger side of a P76 car with the door open, talking to some fat-arsed pro.

I had with me a pair of pliers. There is an art to using a pair of pliers in a street fight, but I won't go into that. I punched approximately 30 puncture wounds into the Turk's face and nearly blinded him – and I did it all in broad daylight while two uniformed police sat 20-feet away in a police car, eating hamburgers.

When Turkish George was a limp, bleeding mess in the gutter, I said to the cops, 'Let's go.' They handcuffed me and I was in the back of the police car when the ambulance arrived to take Turkish George away.

I was released on bail on my own reconnaissance after

being charged with grievous bodily harm. It appears that the police hated Turkish George and thought his injuries were poetic justice. At my trial, the magistrate asked if there was anything I wanted to say. I said, 'Yes, I am only sorry I didn't blind the bastard completely.'

I pleaded guilty, and got two years. Big deal.

I was told later in jail by a junkie who knew St Kilda well that the little blonde girl didn't return to Fitzroy Street. It was well worth two years.

Sydney may have all the razzle dazzle but most of the deadly serious work gets done in Melbourne. There is no doubt it is the unofficial murder capital of Australia.

In fact, I believe that in the State of Victoria there would be between 25 and 50 murders a year that never see the light of day.

Australia is a big country and shovels are cheap. Victoria may be the garden state but if you dug it up, you would find a heap of bodies. The garden probably grows so well because of all the blood and bone that has been spread over it.

If a crook goes missing in Melbourne chances are he isn't on holiday at Surfers Paradise. Anybody who adds up the numbers over the last 100 years will see I am right. Victoria is the state of the big vanish.

It is generally believed that I got the nickname 'Chopper' because I cut my ears off; but that isn't right. I got the name when I was a kid after a character in a cartoon strip. The name Chopper has nothing to do with my ears being cut off. The cartoon was called Chopper and Yakkie. There was a big dog which used to protect a little duck from a fox. I was nicknamed after the dog. Few people know that.

The other thing they don't know is that I didn't cut my own ears off at all. The man who cut them off was Kevin James Taylor, the chap doing life for shooting Pat Shannon. If a man tries to cut his own ears off he will make a pig's breakfast of the job, so I asked Kevin to do it for me. I went into the Number One shower yard of H Division, sat down, folded my arms and sat as still as I could.

Kevin had the razor blade. I said, 'OK, do it.' He started to do it really gently and slow, but that was very painful. I said, 'Come on, you bloody fairy, rip into it,' and so he did.

I remember the sound, it was like running your fingernails down a blackboard at school, only it was going through my head, then I felt the warm blood bubbling in my ears. Then he did the second one. I thought Van Gogh had done it, so it couldn't be life-threatening. I decided to have a cold shower and all the bleeding would stop. But it just wouldn't slow at all.

The blood flowed and flowed after the ears came off; the rest of the guys freaked out, they thought I'd gone crazy. Kevin knocked on the yard door and the screws let me out. We all said I'd cut my ears off because we didn't want to get Kevin into trouble. He's out now, so it doesn't matter.

The doctors didn't believe me, but when I looked down on the ground at my fallen ears, I was sure I could see them doing an Irish Jig. Maybe I was seeing things or maybe it was the nerves in the ears making them twitch. When I got to hospital I was in a state of temporary insanity. I remember being pushed on a trolley towards the operating table. I could swear that Billy 'The Texan' Longley, my good friends 'Sammy' Hutchinson and Johnny 'The Face' Morrison, who had been dead for years, were pushing the trolley. I asked who was doing the operation and Sammy said, 'Don't worry, Chopper, I am.' I screamed and then went into surgery. I saw a screw from H Division, Billy Parker. He was all in green with a mask on. I asked him who was doing the operation and he said he was. The next thing I woke up after surgery and I am glad to say most of it was a bad dream.

Why did I have my ears chopped off? I had just been to the classification board and I said I didn't want to be in H Division. And they said: 'You will remain in H Division until you are released. You are not getting out of H Division.'

I was the head of the Overcoat Gang and we were at war with virtually the rest of the jail at the time and they didn't want me in the mainstream of the jail.

I told them, 'I will be leaving H Division, tomorrow.' They said, 'No, you won't,' and I said I would. So I went back and got Kevin to cut my bloody ears off. You reckon I didn't leave H Division straight away? The classo board nearly came down and carried me out themselves.

The first time it happened it was big news, then everyone started doing it, nothing to do with me. Then all the nutcases in here thought there was something to be gained out of this. I was the president of the Van Gogh club until Garry David cut his penis off. I wrote to him, 'You can take over.' When the dicky birds start hitting the pavement I thought it was time to resign.

Enduring a bit of pain is one thing, but that's a bit much.

FAST EDDY

Fast Eddy got grabbed on a Friday night,
He died on Sunday lunch,
I didn't use much violence,
I didn't kick or punch,
But we had some fun before he died,
Yes we had some fun,
Played a game called kneecap,
Kneecap nail gun,
I had to keep Eddy fresh,
He spent five days in a fridge,
Until I could arrange his funeral,
Under West Gate Bridge,
Fast Eddy had a heap of gold,
And every ounce of it I sold,
Eddy had a heap of dash,

But not enough to keep his cash,
He made it all from selling dope,
But in the end, he had no hope,
His mother wonders where Eddy is,
She cries and feels blue,
But don't cry dear, this is just a poem,
And poems are rarely true.
Ha Ha.

Chapter 8

Life on the Inside

'It appears that the murder, rape and abduction of children has become the Australian national pastime ... the hangman, and only the hangman, can end this foul practice.'

YOU will notice that I have not written about the horrors of prison life, or the conditions, hardships, treatment and so forth, because men reading this book who have been to jail will be bored to tears and people who haven't been to jail can bloody well come in here and find out for themselves.

I may have had a niggle here and there along the way but I haven't gone into vivid detail. Most of the time it is a very boring place. Some prisoners like to waffle on about the dark and lonely solitude of their damp and lonely cell and how they never forgot the sound of the cell door slamming for the first time. What a load of crap. One cell is the same as any other. When you have heard one cell door slam you have heard them all. Jail life can be summed up in two words: petty and boring.

The day-to-day regulations are petty and drawn up by

head office nitwits. After the years that I have done inside I would write 1,000 pages on jail life. But men who have done it, lived it, bled it, cried and nearly died in it, couldn't be bothered.

I'll leave that all to one-month wonders, who can write a gripping thriller based on their blood-chilling adventures in Her Majesty's Motel. Who mentioned Derryn Hinch? Most of the men who have written about prisons would be frightened by a day trip to the Old Melbourne Jail and most of the people who write about crime and punishment wouldn't recognise a criminal if they got shot in the arse by Ned Kelly.

Some of these so-called experts make me laugh. They are a veritable font of knowledge. They wouldn't know what they are talking about. They wouldn't know a crook if they woke up to find Marlon Brando trying to put a horse's head in their bed.

I suspect that the only knowledge any of them has is that he has read every crime book that has ever been published and he knows Bob Bottom on a first-name basis. Another one once spoke to Julian Knight. Well, let me tell you, I've also spoken to Julian and it is not one of the great insights into the criminal mind.

God save us from all the experts.

Just because a man is sent to prison does not end his interests in the crime world. Certain drug kingpins and upmarket drug dealers still operate and control their businesses from behind bluestone walls. A host of bank robberies are planned, put together and ordered from behind bars and carried outside by friends or helpers.

The amount of crime that is carried out on the orders of men serving sentences is amazing. The amount of crime controlled from behind prison walls would stagger most people. Most drugs deals outside are done over the telephone, so what's the problem? Over the years half the nutcases in Melbourne have consulted me in prison re killing this one or that one, how to make a body vanish, arson, kidnapping, extortion and a host of other serious crimes. I might add, I won't enter into anything, or advise anyone unless it is related to the criminal world itself.

There are petty criminal vendettas and gang wars going on all the time and sooner or later one of the sides comes to me. I have advised both sides on how to kill each other without either side knowing it. I only enter into these things every now and again and I find it to be a good mental exercise and nine times out of ten there is a good drink (payment) in it for me.

The average crook involved in these criminal war situations has no flair or imagination. If they are prepared to listen and follow my advice I'll help.

I love a good criminal war or battle situation and I am only ever consulted on matters of violence and death.

I do believe that anyone stupid enough to be convicted of murder deserves to hang. However, for all the limp wrists who think that hanging is a barbaric page of history from the dark ages some conditions should be made.

I believe the penalty should be re-introduced for anyone offending against children. Anyone who has kidnapped, raped or murdered a minor, if convicted, should be hanged. No question. Anyone who disagrees with that, in my opinion, bears watching. Anyone who would not applaud the death penalty for such offences is suspect.

It appears that the murder, rape and abduction of children has become the Australian national pastime. The hangman and only the hangman can bring an end to this foul practice.

Just because I am a criminal, or should I say a retired one, doesn't mean I agree with the actions of the human filth who offend against children. As for the hangman, if I had been convicted of murder I would have saved him the trouble and necked myself.

I am the only crook I have heard of who believes in hanging. On my right forearm I have these words tattooed, 'who dares wins', 'Kamikazi' and 'Bushido'. A host of so-called tough guys say they believe in these words, but will not live up to them.

I have always kept suicide as my final option, the final laugh at my enemies who feel that they have defeated me. A man who doesn't fear death, who holds his own life as an option, a man willing to take his own life in the face of final defeat, cannot be beaten.

My enemies have fallen, weakened and run because they have placed more importance on their own lives than I did. Don't misunderstand, I don't want to die. I want to live as long as God allows. But I don't fear death. As long as my death has a certain amount of style, flair and dash involved, I don't mind.

A life sentence in jail, is to my mind, the final defeat, the final laugh on me and I couldn't take that. I would have no way out except to take my own life. I would welcome the hangman. I don't think there is a sadder, more lonely lost sight than the face of a man who has just been given a life sentence. Everyone I know in the criminal world will disagree with me here but as far as I am concerned the hangman is kinder than old age in prison.

I haven't spoken much about jail and the mental and emotional effect that long years in H Divison and Jika have had on me. It has numbed my senses, no one could ever judge what I am feeling from the expression on my face as I would smile at my own mother's funeral.

A smile is just my natural look most of the time. I have found myself carrying on conversations with myself and the screws and other inmates sometimes catch me at it much to my embarrassment. The worrying thing is that I quite enjoy these personal chats with myself; there is no possible chance of disagreements and I always make a lot of sense.

I am a bit lucky that the blows to the head I have received over the years have done something to my timing. I can be in jail for years and years and the time doesn't seem to mean much. It is a bit worrying, but it may have done me a favour.

The Australian penal system is a sick, corrupt, drug-infested cesspit of mental illness, perversion and despair where violence is part of daily routine.

Violence is accepted as part of life inside. The RSPCA would put down animals if they had to suffer the kind of mental and physical torment I've seen some of the poor bastards in here go through.

But hard rules apply behind the bluestone walls. They may be sick and sorry rules, but they are the rules of the wild. The strong rule and the weak cry. The criminal world, both inside and outside jail, is ruled through strength. It is not a democracy.

In my opinion, the prison system is lost. No government body can rescue it. All ideas have been tried and all have failed. I have always believed that criminals sentenced to penal servitude are a sad waste of manpower. I once wrote to the then Minister of Defence, Mr Jim Killen, putting forward the suggestion of a punishment battalion. It would work along these lines: any convicted male prisoner sentenced to longer than five years, providing he was in fair health, would serve, or could volunteer to serve, his time in a para-military punishment battalion.

Prisoners from all around Australia would be transferred to the battalion, which would be stationed in outback Northern Territory. Any escape in that heat, with no towns for about 300km, would mean death.

France once had a punishment battalion. Throughout history, various countries have had punishment battalions. Australia needs a fighting edge, and a punishment battalion would give it one – a savage one, at that.

I think that such a battalion should be run on strict military lines. There would be no provision for any outside visitors. I believe that under the rules a prisoner would be able to write and receive letters, and could make a phone call when granted permission.

Corporal punishment, including the use of the birch or cane, would be used. Each man would be given a uniform clearly identifying him as part of the battalion. Each man would be drilled and trained and any breach of standing orders or discipline would mean a sound thrashing with a cane and a day in the hot sun.

They would be under the training of military personnel and knocked into shape, trained in bush survival, physical fitness and combat. All weapons would be locked away when not needed for training. Any attempt at revolt would result in death before a firing squad. The matter would be heard, not by a civil court, but a punishment battalion court martial.

Any area where there was a sign of trouble, the government could send the punishment battalion. You may think they would desert – but in the Foreign Legion, desertion meant death from the enemy, or court martial and death if caught by your own side.

It may sound harsh, but any man who volunteered for the punishment battalion would sign his life over in writing to abide by the rules and regulations.

When this group was put into action, the natural blood lust would take over, they would know they couldn't run and hide so they would fight and kill and create chaos and havoc. It would be their only option.

The Defence Department wrote back saying it was a good idea but was too savage and would cost too much. No doubt they were fobbing me off as just another nutcase, which maybe I am.

However, a battalion of desperate criminally-minded men armed in a combat situation, in a foreign land, have proved through history to conduct themselves in a blood-crazy manner. No army likes to think of a punishment battalion on the other side against them.

Killers, rapists, thieves and armed robbers – trained, armed and placed in the frontline of combat – would prove a blood-crazy force of butchers. When cowards have no place to run, they will drink the blood of 1,000 heroes to survive. Those words were used to describe the Foreign Legion 100 years ago. A punishment battalion is a sound idea, like it or not. It would give a hard edge to the Australian Army and solve a social problem.

A life sentence could be changed to ten years in the punishment battalion.

It's obvious that when war comes it will come as a shock to this disbelieving nation, and we will be caught totally off-guard.

If we become an independent republic we had better be able to defend ourselves. As it is now we had better give all the girl guides a pocket knife each, for if we don't do something, that is all we'll end up with.

I may be a crook, but I'm a patriotic crook.

Chapter 9

The Overcoat War

*'I am confident that I hold the bashing record inside Pentridge
... and it will never be beaten.'*

THE Overcoat Gang War, which went five years inside Pentridge, was probably the bloodiest crime war in Victoria. But because it was waged inside jail very little was ever heard about it on the outside.

Like most wars, it started over something fairly small ... in this case, when Piggy Palmer accused me of eating the Christmas sausages in H Division. The word was out in 1975 that we would get a feed – I think two each – of thick pork sausages. Everyone was looking forward to them, and I was in charge of bringing the food up.

When it got there ... no sausages.

Palmer said I had eaten the lot. Well, there would have been 60 sausages and I was supposed to have eaten all of them. I love a snag but that's ridiculous. But, ridiculous or not, harsh words were spoken and blood enemies were made. Keithy Faure sided with Palmer and the war began.

Keith George Faure represented the power in Pentridge in the 1970s. Every Painter and Docker in the jail backed Keithy. He represented the criminal version of the old school tie. Johnny Palmer was also from an old Dockie family so they stuck together. We used to call Keith 'The Frenchman' and we called his crew of underlings and hangers-on the 'KGB', short for Keith George's Boys.

The Overcoat Gang should never have won the war but we did because I never fight anyone at their game, on their playing field, with their rules.

Keith lost the war with me because he spent too much time trying to be a politician. Once the blood starts flying, politics and talk won't solve anything. But while old Keithy didn't know much about tactics, he did have guts, that's for sure.

Besides the Great Christmas Sausage Scandal, there was another underlying reason for the war. Faure ran the Dockies in jail and I was close to Billy 'The Texan' Longley. He wanted Longley's head on a plate and he would have been happy to do a life sentence to get at 'The Texan'.

During Longley's sentence it was made clear to one and all that you don't kill 'The Texan' unless you kill 'Chopper' first, because my revenge would have been tenfold and I would have drowned the offenders in their own blood. It saddens me that Old Billy did not appreciate that the Overcoat Gang kept him alive when he was in jail. Does he really think he stayed alive in there because of his own physical abilities?

During the five-year war the Overcoat Gang was out-numbered, but I had a blood-crazy crew who threw themselves into their work with admirable zeal.

Some members came and went but the main players were my good self, Jimmy Loughnan, now dead, Johnny Price, who committed suicide, Danny James, who has been declared criminally insane, Ted Eastwood, still in jail, Bluey B, in jail, Paul Hetzel, expelled for cowardice in the face of the enemy (and later became a crown witness in the Russell Street bombing case) and Amos 'The Witchdoctor' Atkinson, who is alive and free.

The bash list during the war was astounding. For some time we kept count. My personal list was 63 attacks and 11 attempted murders.

Amos got about 30, Jimmy Loughnan iron-barred his fair share – God knows, I would say about 20. The list was very long. Johnny Price had his own list. Then Jim teamed up with Robbie Wright and they scored a few more.

I would say the Overcoat War saw well over 100 separate attacks over the five years before some of us went to Jika and couldn't get at each other as often.

I am confident that I hold the bashing record inside Pentridge and it will never be beaten, because the jail is now structured differently.

The war ended in 1980 because they sent some of us to Jika Jika when it first opened. There were a few halfhearted attempts to keep it going but we just couldn't get at each other any more.

Prisoner violence was considered the pastime of the 1970s. Back then some of the screws and the governors encouraged it. They thought it was akin to a bloody good football match. It kept the prison population busy and gave them something to think about.

The jail governors today are a little limp-wristed when it comes to matters of violence. Since the 1980s the jail has been ruled by drugs and violence, but the class of men and the class of violence is very petty. Savage and evil, yes, but very petty.

In the 1970s the jail was ruled by home brew and iron bars. The violence raged from one end of the place to the other. The Press got told very little about it. The younger crims today simply find it hard to believe the stories of blood and guts that went on inside and outside jail.

These days the so-called top crims are so full of junk they couldn't change their underwear. Outside it is the same. The gang bosses and the drug lords get rid of their enemies by ringing the police. They demand police protection if their own lives are threatened. The guts and courage have gone. The criminal scene is just a sea of vomit. But back in the days of the Overcoat War there was plenty of full-on guts and courage on both sides.

Our side was outnumbered but we had some great tactical advantages. We had a spy network right through the prison and we had the moral support and the blind eye encouragement of a handful of the most right-wing, broken-nosed, cauliflower-eared, hired by the pound, knuckles scraping on the ground, leg-breaking screws any jail had ever seen. We also had one big bonus, the blessing of Jimmy Quinn, the Pentridge Governor of Security.

When the blood starts flying, I'll do business with the Devil himself. Victory at all costs is the only thing. You can discuss the moral ethics as we bury the enemy. That's how I got away with it all for five years: I had a friend in high places.

Governor Quinn died in the early 1980s. He was a grand old fellow, a man who would have a drink on any occasion. He loved a bet, a fight, and blood and guts – and he thought the world of me and I of him. In the 1970s Jimmy Quinn once had his nose broken in a punch-on with Keithy Faure in B Division. So when the Overcoat War broke out, Jimmy Quinn took my side. Faure already had a few high-ranking prison staff on side, but I had all the old-time blood and guts brigade. After all, it was a prison war between inmates, but we were fighting on the screws' playing field, so some friends at court were needed on both sides. I think Keithy Faure went through the whole war wishing he hadn't broken the governor's nose.

Through Governor Quinn I could get into other prisoners' cells at night, get into other yards, and get prisoners transferred from one division to another, have my own men moved. The pull I had was quite unbelievable. Quinn used to send two security screws down to H Division early in the morning, handcuff me and bring me up to the security office and into his office. I'd be uncuffed there and the governor would sit down with me, his office door closed, and we'd drink coffee and eat Choc Royal bikkies and watch slides of his latest overseas holidays. Now and again he would break out a small bottle of whisky or a can or two of beer. At the height of the Overcoat War he once had me brought to his office and over a can of beer he explained to me that for every dozen or so bashings and attacks the Overcoat Gang did, only one would get a mention on any report, and none, if any, on my personal records. It was getting a bit tropical and I had to ease it up for a while. The A Division bomb had just gone off and Quinn was under pressure. He then said that every twelve or so bashings one would get a mention.

When I cut my ears off Governor Quinn came to hospital to visit me. When I got stabbed he also came in to see me. He was good mates with my dad. He was not a corrupt man. He was just an old-style blood and guts boy, and a good war in jail gave us all something to do. He was a grand old fellow, and his death was a great sadness to me personally.

The toughest screw in Pentridge throughout the 60s and 70s was old George. He was an H Division screw and as hard as nails, but a goodhearted fellow. A former European boxing title-holder, a prisoner of the Germans for three years and a defector from the Russian Navy, George was not a man to be taken lightly. He was another old-style blood and guts boy and considered a good jail war was just what the boys needed to keep busy. He was a great old chap and no longer in the prison service. They were a breed of tough prison officers with a sense of humour – men who got respect, but who were not corrupt.

One of Jimmy Loughnan's favourite party tricks in H Division during the war was to get hold of chaps we felt had been 'putting holes in their manners'. We would grab the offending party and give him a touch-up – otherwise known as a sound beating. Then we would stand him up. I'd put a butcher's knife to his neck and Jimmy would pop a razor blade in his mouth and he would be told to chew on it.

There would be a little protest at first, but it was a case of chew or die – and a mouth full of blood was better than a neck full of cold steel. So chew, it would be. If you've never seen a man chew a razor blade you have never seen blood flow. There would be choking and coughing and blood – sometimes vomiting. It was a lesson once learnt, never forgotten. It must have been pain beyond description. But H Division in the 1970s was a bloodsoaked mental hospital of violence and more violence – and only the truly ultra-violent could rule it.

Loughnan had a true blood lust. As a 14-year-old boy he was placed in J Ward at Ararat – a mental hospital for the criminally insane. J Ward is still a dark legend today in the minds of the men who have been in it.

Now, I certainly can't admit to this, so I will have to

dismiss it as foul gossip and slander. I'm referring to the bomb that went off in a cell in A Division in the late 1970s. I've done that much jail I can't remember even the date and the year. Johnny Palmer and Neil Bugg and some other chap got caught in it. A young chap called Trevor Taylor came down to H Division from A Division over suspicion of planting the bomb. It didn't kill anyone but nearly did. It was suggested that Jimmy Loughnan told Trevor to plant the bomb on my orders. I believe it was a 'fertiliser bomb'. Of course, I deny all. It was rumoured to be another strike in the Overcoat War. I met poor Neil a few years later; I had nothing against him, but he was a casualty of war.

The list of weapons made and used in Pentridge goes on and on, and we used them all. There are iron bars, claw hammers, garden spades, home-made tomahawks, ice picks, screwdrivers sharpened to a pinpoint, nunchukkas, meat cleavers and butcher's knives from the kitchen.

My favourite was a razor blade welded into the end of a toothbrush with a cigarette lighter, or a blade with sticky-tape wrapped around one end. When it is held between the thumb and the forefinger with a flash of the wrist you can open a man's face up like a ripe watermelon.

Pepper tossed in the eyes can blind an enemy for a short time. The toilet or shower attack is a favourite in jail: taking an enemy as he sits on the toilet or is under the shower. Dennis Allen got his while he was under the shower. The

Top: Baby Read,1955, aged 7 months, at the Methodist Babies' Home, Melbourne.

Below left: My Dad, Keith.

Below right: One of my many visits inside.

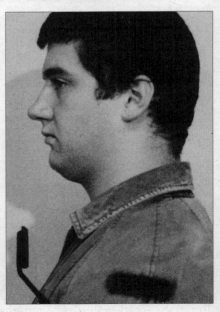

READ M.B.
1·7·11·54 DKT 3337·74
A.R.S 46.78

Top left: My home away from home: HM Prison, Pentridge.

Top right: In my H division cell in 1990.

Below: 1978 mugshots.

**Tooled up and
ready for action.**

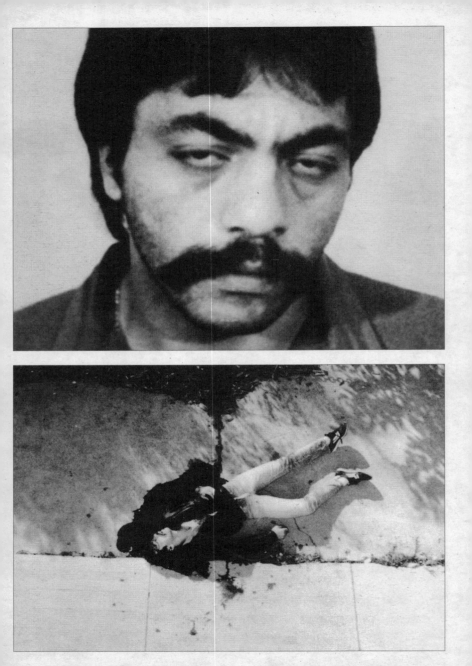

Siam 'Sammy the Turk' Ozerkam, alive and dead. I shot him in self defence outside Bojangles nightclub in Melbourne.

The CHOPPER READ file

MARK BRANDON Read — "Chopper" to his friends and enemies — is one of the most dangerous men in Australia.

A brutal criminal who wanted to be a policeman, he has turned himself into an out-of-control bounty hunter. A man who calmly stalks criminals, killing, shooting and bashing as he sees fit.

Poet, comic, standover man, killer, manipulator and gun freak, "Chopper" Read is disliked by police and hated by most of the underworld.

He is a loose cannon who routinely betrays anyone if he can find an advantage for himself. But both inside and outside jail, he treats life and death as one great joke. In the first of two reports, JOHN SILVESTER profiles the life of a crazy killer.

BOUNTY HUNTER

BELOW: Mark Brandon Read . . . a gun at his head, he always jokes about death.

THIS is the story of one of Australia's most violent men — a man distilled and distrusted on both sides of the law. Mark Brandon "Chopper" Read is a criminal who has declared war on the underworld.

A killer who always wanted to be a policeman, he has become, in his own mind, a one-man army — The Bounty Hunter.

"Chopper" Read admits to having instigated 63 bashings and 11 attempted murders while in jail.

Some say he is mad; others say just plain bad.

But behind the smiling violence is a complex, cunning individual who has maintained a campaign of terror, both inside and outside jail, for more than a decade.

He has mutilated himself, but scared many others.

Read claims that he would never harm a law-abiding citizen and would rather take on criminals and live off them.

In a statutory declaration written by Read, he said: "I have always believed that it is a total waste of time to rob a bank when I can rob a bank robber.

"I have an image within the Melbourne underworld as a toe-cutter — a man who stands over other criminals for their money.

"I have never turned my hand in a criminal manner to anyone not already involved in the criminal world.

"I am a very hated man within the Melbourne underworld — a hatred being borne out of fear."

Read, 35, was released from Bendigo Jail in 1986 after establishing a reputation as one of the toughest men behind bars.

It was strange — he was liked by many prison officers, but detested and feared by fellow inmates. He was an informer who survived.

IN the previous decade, Read had emerged from being a two-bit hood to a figure who made the toughest crooks think twice before crossing him.

He first came to notice as a man who stood over drug dealers. One of his old tricks was to rob a pusher's drugs down the lavatory and then steal the money.

He once applied to join the police force. He was rejected — because he had flat feet.

Read once used a shotgun to try to kidnap a County Court judge in a bid to have a prisoner, Jimmy Loughnan, released from jail.Loughnan was one of five prisoners who later perished in the Jika Jika fire.

In separate incidents, Read cut his ears off while in jail, used oxy-acetylene gear to try to burn off a tattoo on his arm and stabbed himself in the eyes with a cigarette.

He was seriously injured when he was stabbed by a prisoner and complimented his foe for "having a terrific sneak go" before realising that blood was pouring from the injuries.

A prison officer once struck him over the head at least 15 times, before the baton broke, during a Pentridge riot in 1978. Read then continued to strike himself on the head with a piece of wood.

Read was the leader of Pentridge's notorious "overcoat gang" — a group of prisoners who wore long grey coats which concealed weapons they used to bash fellow inmates. When Read was finally released, after serving more than nine years of a 14-year sentence for the attempted kidnap of the judge, he made immediate contact with members of the armed robbery squad.

A DAY later Mark Brandon Read, one of the toughest men in the underworld met police at the Bush Inn, in Toorak, and made a startling offer. He wanted to be their informer.

He was given the code name "Melville" because he promised to gather information on Australia's then most wanted criminal Russell "Mad Dog" Cox, whose real name is Melville.

Read turned out to be a super informer for police. He provided information which resulted in the arrest and conviction of several major crooks and the seizure of drugs, guns and stolen property.

But "Chopper" Read was not motivated by the spirit of some hidden good. He had informed his own war against the underworld and was prepared to use anything in his power to get results.

Armed robbery squad detectives had a top informer who had a wide network of contacts. But the detectives were to pay a huge price for the information.

Mark Read . . . hacked his ears off while in jail and now refers to himself as "The best looking bloke with no ears in Pentridge."

PAGE EIGHT

The thoughts of Chairman Chopper

MARK Brandon Read hardly fits the image of a philosopher.

But the following "Thoughts According To Chopper" suggest he might be something of a criminal Confucius:

"Paranoia is the criminal equivalent for intelligence."

"Just because you're going to kill a man is no reason for bad manners."

"A man's history is the facts agreed upon by his victims."

"Think before you act — but act before they think."

"Put your faith in Allah but keep your camels tied."

"The hole has already been dug for me — so a wise old Sicilian bandit once said. My enemies, I fear not, but heaven protect me from my friends."

"I'd stab myself in the guts for $50,000."

On his regret about not killing a former friend:

"It was only my soft heart that pulled me up from shooting . . . the inside of a tree shredder headfirst — I came live to regret my Christian kindness."

On someone about violence in society:

"I've noticed in the time everybody wants everybody killed. But getting a heavy prison out of the weak person" . . .

prior to the event is like pulling teeth."

Regarding repeated allegations of police corruption he made: "We are slowly going to drive these nitwits out of their minds."

"They can't bluff me or frighten me with the thought of long jail — I run the jail — ha, ha. I'm quite happy to do any amount of jail if I can expose certain corrupt police and they can't deal with that so they call me mad, insane and so on. But still I say, get it to court. Ha, ha, we will slowly drive these nitwits off their heads."

On a man he intends to kill: "I will come after him like a mad kamikaze pilot."

Read is also searching of a poet:

"Mr Asia rose and fell, Bandalli rests in hell, Nande Hoh died in Spain. But on the streets it's hell — little pain.

The guns clatter, the bodies splatter, Heads get smashed and kneecaps shatter. Corruption under control, that's you in the sky. We never get to heaven. With a fill, I don't care if it rains or freezes, As long as I've got my plastic Jesus, Sitting on the dashboard of my car."

TOMORROW: Underworld targets 'Chopper'

Fame at last! A 1990 feature on me.

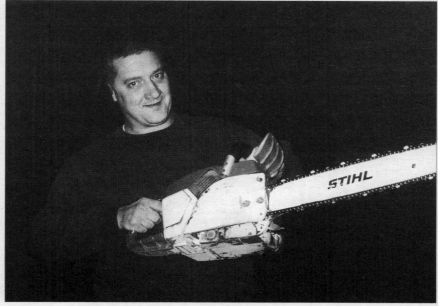

Top: Thank God for gel!

Below: The trusty chainsaw.

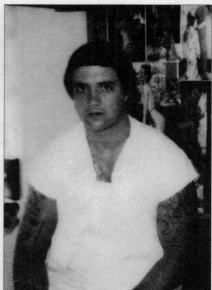

Top left: Nick the Greek: I shot him and burned his house down – so what?

Top right: Portrait of the artist as a young gunman.

Below: I never go outdoors without my sunglasses.

ordinary ballpoint pen jabbed into the eye ball, a tin of condensed milk put in two thick socks makes a lethal cosh, broken glass put into the victim's food, razor blades in his bed, caustic soda in a cordial bottle, razor blades buried in a bar of soap. The fun and games in here never end; tactics are only limited by your imagination.

Once, during the war, it was decided someone had to go up to B Division from H Division and bash a couple of blokes. Jimmy Loughnan had to remain on H Division on punishments. I wasn't allowed out of H Division as I was a maximum security prisoner, so it was between Johnny Price and Amos Atkinson.

Amos and Price drew straws – matchsticks, in fact. Amos got the short stick. He went up to B Division after asking for a transfer out of H Division. He walked into B Division – didn't even put his things in his cell – and got a big hammer and bashed Lance Chee and Graeme Jensen over the head, then came back down to H Division.

That was all very well. The trouble was, I'd sent him up to B Division to bash two other chaps. I was a little bit put out. I said to Amos: 'What have Chee and Jensen got to do with anything?'

I don't believe this, but this was his answer: 'All white guys look a bit alike'. Rubbish. He was just being lazy, that's all. That was 1979. He was charged internally over it at Governor's Court. I never sent him on any other seek and destroy missions. All white guys look alike! What a lot of codswallop. Seven years later Jensen and his stupid crew tried to attack me over that, and came unstuck.

One trick we used that I can now admit was the soap scam. A dirty trick but it was a jail gang war, so all was fair ...

I got a dozen bars of soap, soaked them in a plastic bucket of hot water for 15 minutes, then pulled them out and slid a razor blade down the side of each bar. Then I left them out in the sun to harden.

I was H Division number one billet at the time. My job was serving out the meals, cleaning the cells, the wing, the labour yard and the shower yards – meaning I had total run of the division. I removed all soap from the shower yards; and put six blocks of my special trick soap in each shower yard.

Needless to say, without going into the bloody details, it worked a treat. My enemies were not only frightened to eat their food – for fear of rat poison or human shit in the stew – they couldn't even use soap in the showers without fear. I was mentally destroying their will. I would leave dobs of jam under their beds to attract ants. I'd piss in their cordial bottles, shit in their jam and cover it with jam. Along with the bloody violence and the physical beatings these added touches reduced Faure's gang to tears – and total surrender.

When I was in B Division in 1975 they let us put on concerts and shows in B Division and A Division. The B Division boys went down to the A Division concert. Me and Jimmy Loughnan were both wearing overcoats: me with a tomahawk and Jimmy with a knife and an iron bar.

We got to see the best concert ever – Johnny O'Keefe. He sang all his songs. He came dressed as if he was playing a big show and not a jail concert. He was a real professional and it was a privilege and a pleasure just to sit and watch him. Me and Jim sat up front with a couple of our boys watching our backs.

After the show a Sydney crim who Jimmy knew was talking to Johnny O'Keefe and called us over. So we got to meet JOK. For me it was a great moment. He was a fantastic fellow. And there was a beautiful female singer who also sang for us – Dianna Lee – a lovely blonde lady. We all shook hands and Jimmy got a kiss on the cheek. Johnny O'Keefe was a real knockabout to talk to – and knew quite a few crooks. I guess big stars like him know a million people. Anyway, as we walked away, my tomahawk dropped down from my belt and fell out under my overcoat and clanged on the floor.

Nobody said anything for a long moment, and then Johnny said, dry as you like, 'I'm bloody glad you liked the show, Chopper ... I wouldn't want to be here if you didn't.' Everyone roared with laughter.

His death was a great loss. He was a top bloke.

Chapter 10

Betrayed

'To be stabbed by the same bloke that I tried to get out of jail is a good lesson ... but a hard way to learn.'

While most of the underworld hated Read, he did have his allies. The man who was his closest friend for many years was armed robber, escaper and violent criminal, James Richard Loughnan.

Loughnan was Read's lieutenant in the Overcoat Gang. They were inseparable. They hatched revenge plots together, and even tried to break out of jail as a team. Loughnan escaped from Pentridge twice and broke both his ankles in a third bid. He was serving 12 years for armed robbery during the height of the prison war.

After one escape in 1974, Loughnan was shot in the back by Box Hill gunsmith, Gordon MacDonald, during a failed armed robbery attempt. In 1978 Loughnan, Read and John Price escaped from H Division and sat on the roof of A Division in a jail protest.

In 1977 while Loughnan was recovering from his broken ankle in H Division, Read was released from jail. He had *promised Loughnan he would hatch a plot to get him released. Read marched into the County Court in early 1978 and held Judge Martin hostage at gunpoint, demanding the release of his friend. It was a plan even Read knew was doomed to fail before he began.*

For his show of loyalty Read was sentenced to another 13 years jail. Ironically, the friendship was soured when Loughnan stabbed Read in H Division when even he thought Read was going too far in the Overcoat Gang war.

Read said later that after the stabbing he vowed he would never fully trust another man.

Loughnan was one of five inmates who burnt themselves to death in the Jika Jika Division fire in October 1987.

When Jimmy Loughnan, Johnny Price and I broke out of H Division a prison officer hit me over the head 15 or 20 times before the baton broke. I said, 'You'd better carve me up, Jim, I'll go to J Ward Ararat. If you put enough blood on me yourself, then the screws won't bother flogging me.'

Looking back, it was a very foolish thing to hand a psychopath a razor blade and ask him to carve me up. He went in so deep it nearly went through to my lungs.

He was a friend of mine, poor old Jim. He died in that Jika fire. What people don't know is that he was one of two people who stabbed me: he ended up turning on me.

There was an ice pick and a knife used in the attack on me. Poor old Jim hung the ice pick in, but he's dead now so it doesn't matter.

Loughnan was a hard man, a real hard man; he was in my gang years ago. Maybe I was going a bit too crazy for them. Back in those days there was a rather mad plan hatched by the Overcoat Gang to literally take over H Division.

We were going to grab the whole division. There was me, Jimmy Loughnan and Amos Atkinson. We were going to take over the division because every enemy we had at the time was in the division in 1979.

We had ice picks, knives, everything. I said right, we'll grab the whole division, we'll lock all the prison officers up in the scullery, and we won't hurt any of them.

This was just after I attacked that judge, so I had 17 years to think about it. I was only 24, young and crazy. I said we'll take the whole division over, then we'll grab the keys and go to every cell, pull each enemy out one at a time, and we'll deal with them.

We were going to deal with them in no uncertain terms, short of death. Anyway, they went away and had a chat about it. Amos Atkinson and Jimmy Loughnan and another bloke. And they came up with the theory that the old Chopper's gone crazy.

The next day I stepped into the yard and that was it: Amos Atkinson bailed out of the yard. He had held hostages at the Italian Waiters' club and demanded my release from H Division, and so still couldn't go all the way against me. He wouldn't turn on me, but at the same time he wouldn't warn me that I was going to be attacked either, so he got out of the yard.

They really didn't have the courage to come to me and say: 'No, we don't want to be in it.' If they had said: 'No, we don't want to be in it,' I would have said 'All right,' but they thought I was so off my head at the time that they couldn't reason with me.

I lost part of my spleen, most of the gall bladder, so many feet of stomach tubing, so many feet of bowel, part of the colon. I got the ice pick in the back of the neck, which nearly severed the spine.

After the operation I was found on the hospital floor doing pushups. You've got to understand that they fill you full of pethidene. The day after, I had stitches everywhere, tubes in my nose, in my arm and in my penis, but I was also as high as a kite on pethidene.

I did do, I think, 30 pushups. I think I re-split the stitches inside my stomach. I did it just to prove that I hadn't been got at. The reason I tell you this, is that no one did a day's jail over the attack. It was declared a case of self-defence and it's now ancient history.

I don't want to say much about Jimmy Loughnan. When I got stabbed in H Division in 1979 I went from an 18-stone giant to a 14-stone weakling overnight.

The treachery of Jimmy's actions that day upset my mental wellbeing and I still remember it as if it was yesterday. The stabbing was nothing. Big deal, you get over that, although I never did regain my physical stature. Prior to that I was 18 stone of rock. To think that I was doing 13 years for trying to get Jimmy out of J Ward Ararat. Ah well.

I saw Jim again in late 1983 when I came up from Jika. I was walking past B Division to go to the clothing store. There was Jimmy, standing in front of B Division. He couldn't fight, but he wasn't a coward, so he stood his ground and braced himself for the expected bashing.

I walked up and kissed him on the cheek and said: 'Don't worry, Jimmy, I'm not going to hurt you. Your own life will destroy you.'

He said: 'Yeah, I know it will.'

As I walked away he called out to me, 'It wasn't personal, Chopper.'

I kept walking and didn't turn back. I had tears in my eyes. Why didn't I kick him into a bleeding jelly? The bloke had been my best friend since 1975. He was my brother. I loved him like a brother. I wasn't angry and I didn't hate him; he just broke my heart.

I saw him once more after that in K Division about two days before the fire. I saw poor Robert Wright the very day before. He said: 'We've got something going, Chopper, you'll love it. It will be good for a laugh.' Poor mad buggers.

The whole reason I went into the court that day and grabbed Judge Martin was all to do with my friendship with Loughnan. I was trying to get Jimmy out of J Ward Ararat. He was writing to me, pleading with me to get him out. I once promised him in H Division, and I always keep a promise to a friend.

He had just escaped from jail and broke both his ankles, when he jumped the fence. He was in the yard there, it was raining, he was crying and his feet were blue, and he thought he was going to lose both his feet. He had four, five or six years to go. I said, 'Listen, Jim, when I get out, give me about six months, then write to me and then I'll come and get you.'

He said, 'You'll be out eating pizzas and drinking beer and you won't want to give that away to help me.' And I said I would. And when he wrote to me, the truth was, he was right, I didn't want to give it all away. I didn't want to attack that judge and it really was a half-hearted effort.

The thing was that I had given my word that I would do it. Back when I was 24, that was very serious to me, that I had sworn, on my friendship to Jimmy Loughnan, that I would try and get him out.

When he wrote to me, I was having a good time. I didn't want to walk away from all that but I had given my word, and I was obliged to go through with it. So I went and did what I did, and naturally I got caught.

If it had worked I was going to surrender myself anyway, so it was certain jail – win, lose or draw. I don't know if I was insane; I can't think on that level now. I had a deep sense of friendship, but over the years the more knives that got stuck in my back and the more times I was betrayed, that sense of friendship becomes less and less.

I remember I was living with a girl named Lindy at the time. I remember kissing her goodbye on that morning and then 'Dave the Jew' drove me to the court.

I went into the County Court building with a shotgun stuffed down the front of my pants. I asked a policeman there which courts were in session. He told me and I walked into the first one I saw. Judge Martin was the first cab off the rank. I climbed on to the judge's bench, put the gun to his head and demanded Jimmy's release. I knew it could never work but I had given my word to try.

I remember after it was all over I wrote to Judge Martin and said I was sorry and he wrote back to me. I no longer have the letters, but it seems I had met him at the Melbourne Cup in November 1977 a few months before. He was very concerned for me and wished me all the very best for the future. I thought that was very nice of him. I had no ill will towards him. It was all to try to get Jimmy Loughnan out of J Ward.

I wouldn't attack a judge now, to get anyone out of jail, because too many people have betrayed me. Too many people have stabbed me in the back. Too much has happened to me. To be stabbed by the same bloke that I tried to get out of jail is a terrible lesson, a good lesson, but a hard way to learn. So the Mark Read of then is not the Mark Read of now. We all grow, don't we?

Jimmy Loughnan escaped quite a few times from Pentridge

simply because he tried so many times. I've only tried once, and I knew it was a stupid idea even before agreeing to go along. No one else would be in it, but I had nothing better to do.

Here is what we did. Me and Jim got ourselves nailed into a small crawl space between the roof of the B Division library and the B Division theatre. We had to then cut our way through the floor of the theatre, cut our way through the bars of the theatre window, climb down then get over the wall.

It sounds simple. We took a bottle of water mixed with cordial, four bags of lollies, some chocolates – and a butcher's knife. We were, by the way, going to cut through the theatre floor with the bloody butcher's knife. It was all so hopeless. We had half a hacksaw blade to cut the bars of the theatre window. And we had to hide in the crawl space, nailed in with no way out except the theatre floor, hiding from the screws. We were supposed to hide for a good 24 hours before we made our move ...

I shook my head when I heard the plan, but went along with it for the sheer hell of it. The things one does in the name of friendship.

We were in the crawl space. The night muster bell rang and the screws were alerted that two were missing. A big search started for us – there were bells ringing, the whole bit.

Jim wanted to take a piss. Then he wanted a lolly. Then he wanted a chocolate, then a drink of cordial. We'd been hiding four hours and Jim had eaten all the supplies, drank half the water and cordial and taken three leaks. And there was hardly any air. What a fiasco.

God, I was glad when they found us.

Postscript. There is a file photograph of old Squizzy Taylor standing next to his bail bondsmen, a Richard James Loughnan. That was Jimmy Loughnan's grandfather.

Jimmy was one of two brothers. His younger brother Glen Loughnan hanged himself in the family shed on the same day Jimmy was shot in Box Hill by gunsmith Gordon MacDonald, or Gordon the Gunnie as Jimmy later called him.

Chapter 11

Toe-cutting

'I have grown to despise and loathe the mainstream criminal population, for they are nothing but weak-gutted mice.'

WHY did I choose to become a toe-cutter, a man who lived by torturing other criminals and robbing them? It is the highest risk area of crime with regard to life and death. But, for a start, I find the selling of drugs to be a girlish, limp-wristed way to earn one's living. It is the wimp's way to gain wealth and power. Why should I steal drugs when I can simply rob the drug seller?

No one ever informs on the toecutter for the crime of torture. They cannot stand up in court against me when they have no feet to stand on – and if they did stand up they would have to be held by the undertaker, because they're all dead. What I have been arrested for are acts of loyalty for fallen comrades, or personal revenge, or acts of underworld violence as a result of war – never for operating as a toecutter.

If you get to the frontline of a war you can be the

safest. As a toecutter, I am hated in the criminal world and everyone wants me dead. But, as I've mentioned before, often the hunted man lives the longest.

The criminal world is a cesspit of vomit. I choose to stay on top of my own ladder, where I can pick my targets more clearly. It is cleaner in the end.

I am not a 'bounty hunter', as I have been called. The criminal term for someone like me is a 'headhunter'. The term 'headhunter' is a purely Australian criminal slang term for someone who lives off the big crooks.

Having spent all my teenage and adult years in the criminal world, both inside and outside prison, I have grown to despise and loathe the mainstream criminal population, for they are nothing but weak-gutted mice. They have no sense of personal honour and courage. The average police dog has more guts and brains than the average member of the criminal world. If there is such a thing as a criminal snob then I am one; I look down my nose at the rest.

People with the drugs and the money call the shots. They have got people working for them who, under normal circumstances, wouldn't urinate on them in the street because the big boss is so weak – but because he has the drug connections and he's got the money he calls the shots. Some weak, insipid, effeminate, despicable character becomes the one who thinks he can run the show.

It makes my stomach turn.

To me toe-cutting, or headhunting, is the cleanest, purest

form of crime, and the headhunter stands alone. The average criminal has the mentality of a pack runner. The headhunter has the mentality of a lone wolf. I will not miss the criminal world or the criminal life. That is why I can walk away and never look back.

In the late 1960s and early 1970s I had been in trouble with the police but I didn't think of myself as a real crim. I was a street fighter and a bloody good one. Then I started to think that I could use that ability to turn over a dollar. I started standing over people who were themselves on the wrong side of the law. It started with the massage parlours and brothels, robbing the blokes who ran the parlours in the early 1970s and robbing the SP bookmakers, the card schools, the gambling clubs and baccarat schools. So much to do and so little time in those days.

The thing was, you'd get into these joints and you'd find rubbish-bin bags full of 'grass', piles of it everywhere. Well, they thought that I was quite funny, because I was ignoring the grass and going for the money. I had a great deal of trouble getting the money out of them − until I got the bright idea of setting fire to their dope. The first time I found heroin in a massage parlour I tipped it out and asked what it was.

There were people literally crying on the floor, on their hands and knees on the floor. I remember once, I had a handful of those red and white caps of heroin and I was throwing them out on to Fitzroy Street, St Kilda, and people were on their hands and knees trying to get them. And I was laughing my head off I couldn't see what it was about.

People who are not on heroin would throw it down the dunny; they would rather have a cup of tea. But for people who are on it or selling it, you would swear that you had taken their mother and thrown her on the street. It's pathetic really.

Drugs were never my go. I wouldn't steal drugs because I would have to re-sell them. All I would have to do is grab the drugs and demand, say, $10,000, or the drugs were down the toilet. It worked all the time. What could the dealer do: go to the coppers and say, 'Big bad Chopper has flushed a kilo of my smack down the dunny'? No way known.

Any criminal who talks about money is a fool. If you have to brag about something, talk about women or the size of your gun, but never discuss financial matters, because if the police or the tax man doesn't overhear your boasting, the toe-cutters surely will. Because I have been full on in crime for the past two decades, my years behind bars have been long. But my time outside, short as it has been, has been very profitable. However, if you want to know whether there is big money in it, the answer is no. After a lifetime of blood and guts torment I haven't got a cracker to my name.

It is bloody pathetic really. I don't have a brass razoo. I have blown it all in less time than it took me to make it. Paying people to keep their mouths shut: wives, girlfriends, sisters and mothers of chaps that I have had run-ins with, pay-offs to get information on targets or as part of revenge campaigns, buying weapons. This is not cheap. Hiring cars, flats, motel rooms, pub rooms, renting places to be used as interrogation rooms, money for shady doctors, financing long-range campaigns, slings and backhanders and repaying debts to friends and helpers. The result is a bit left over for a counter lunch and a few beers while I wonder where it all went.

For example, in 1987, I was standing over ethnic card games in the western suburbs. I would collect about $200 a week from six places. I also collected money from a couple of SP bookmakers, about $200 a week each. I had a handful of massage parlours paying me between $250 to $500 a week, not for protection, but because the parlour bosses wanted me on their side.

I was also collecting a $200- to $300-a-week sling from several Melbourne nightclubs, because the owners wanted to keep me sweet. I had the same arrangement with a few nightclubs in the western suburbs. Basically it worked out to about $3,000 a week in slings, plus my regular standover money I'd pull off other crims. I would average about $5,000 on a good week.

After paying off everyone and everything I would end up with about $2,000 a week for myself, yet I always ended up broke.

Even when I was doing special $20,000 torture jobs, mounting the operation could cost money. The truth is I have always been a very poor money manager. Financially speaking, I was a very small-time crook who tortured millionaire crooks for chicken feed. I was in it more for giggles than gold.

Oh, I'm a crook, all right, but I live off other crims. Within every fish tank there is a shark, within the ocean there are sharks, within the criminal world there are sharks, within any jail there are sharks. What I mean is, if any of these nitwits went over to America they wouldn't last five minutes because there would be a Chopper Read on every tier in every jail. If they went to New York they'd be meeting Chopper Reads on every street corner. They should thank God that they live in Melbourne.

Crims here have been getting around like a protected species. Where's the real harm in what I did? I know that many people, including some police, were quite happy when I dealt out a little bit of 'poetic justice' to some filthy drug pusher. This is what gets me; these crooks have guns and they're willing to put a gun at your head and take your money, willing to beat you to shreds. But if Chopper Read gets them in the lounge room afterwards and nails their hands to a coffee table and says 'where's the money?' they scream 'injustice'. They scream 'foul play'. They scream, 'We're being picked on, we're being tormented and our money is being taken off us.'

Do you honestly think this attitude of 'we're honest crims, you can't come and take our money,' would be tolerated in London, New York or Belfast? What do they scream about me for? What I have done for years is now the accepted thing, because now the crims are feeding off each other. They have become cannibals. The dope dealers are all robbing each other, the bank robbers are robbing each other, the massage parlour owners are standing over each other, the night club owners are standing over and robbing each other.

They see it in on American TV shows and they say, 'Oh gee, that must be the way they are doing it over there; it must be the way to go.' I know it sounds ridiculous but they all try to emulate American television. The number of crims who have got the Scarface video at home would make you laugh.

My reputation in the criminal world has always been based on other people's hatred, fear and paranoia. My image has been made by my enemies, whereas a host of big-name crooks have reputations which come from their friends, admirers and hangers-on. These so-called gangsters have all created images and reputations they don't deserve. But a reputation that has come out of a sea of hatred can be believed. Why would the men who hate someone praise him unless the truth was so overpowermg they had no other choice?

Nothing my enemies say about me can hurt me, as I have no popularity to lose. My friends and loved ones will not fall into a tearful heap on hearing or reading some slander about me, as that is all they have ever heard anyway.

I welcome the news every time I hear that some misguided individual has stated that he will kill me or that there is a contract out on my life or that he knows of men eager to finish me off. For although he doesn't realise it, he is offering me a brilliant plea of self-defence at any future murder trial.

It could be said that the amount of pure naked hatred against me by Crown witnesses at my murder trial and the general feeling of ill-will against me that the jury saw in the court room must have helped me. When a man as hated as me kills then a plea of self-defence is not that hard to accept.

In my enemies rush to condemn me, to destroy me with venom and outrage they have, in fact, almost given me a legal licence to kill – in self-defence of course. The plea of self-defence is rarely used in court and believed even less. In my case it is simply a case of some poor bastard trying to kill Chopper Read again (yawn) as these plots against me are considered commonplace.

If I have so many enemies, who can I trust? As far as trust is concerned, the old saying that there are no friends in business applies a hundred fold in the criminal world. In the name of self-interest and survival most men will betray a friend to save their own skins, or further their own ends. There are a few men who are exceptions to this rule, even fewer in the criminal world.

Chopper's golden rule is that when the shit hits the fan, keep an eye on the people closest to you. The graveyards are full of blokes who got put there by their friends.

All my life I have looked at everything as a fight and I have developed my own theories and opinions about people. I have developed what I have called the Psychology of Fear. I have taken the eye teeth out of every book of tactics, strategy and combat I have read and used what I have learned on the streets and the criminal world. An enemy can cripple itself with its own fear. My Psychology of Fear works because no one knows that I am manipulating the situation to create that fear. Everyone fears the unknown; everyone gets a jump in their hearts out of a bump in the night. Everybody wants to go to heaven but nobody wants to die first.

One of my earliest readings was Dale Carnegie's book *How to Win Friends And Influence People* and I have developed my own twisted version of it. Part of my tactic is to create anger and outrage in the mind and the heart of the enemy, as that is the first and most stupid emotion a man can have. At first you can't hurt an angry, outraged man — but you don't want a cool-headed enemy, either. You must create confusion through mind-numbing misinformation until your target doesn't know what to believe any more. After anger and confusion comes paranoia, and a paranoid enemy is a comedy to watch.

Then, through the use of personal contact via the telephone or even a nice card or flowers you can turn up the heat. Bumping into their old mother with a warm smile and a hello, and asking her to pass on your regards to Sonny Boy. Paranoia and fear combine to create an almost crippled mental state. The war at that stage has been won, and I haven't left my lounge chair.

The actual physical part of this form of combat via a death or act of violence is a small part. It is the very last move on the chess board. I play this game over a period of time to create the maximum tension and stress. If there are drugs at hand, the enemy may partake to steady his nerves. To ease the tension he may take a drink and all the while he is talking and talking about me to his followers, creating further paranoia and panic in the minds of his friends.

What we now have is a heavily armed group of rich and powerful underworld heavies in a state of almost comical paranoia and fear. I like to keep this up for at least a year; all the while I am at ease and they are on guard ready for the pending attack. But the attack doesn't come. Every man or group can only stay in a mental and physical state of siege for so long. In jail, I have seen enemies attempt suicide over this tactic and a few have succeeded. On the outside they may leave the state or offer me gifts of money.

The next step is an act of violence through a night of assorted shootings, never directed at the main target, but at people near and around him. At this point he is ready to give you half, if not all, of what is his. If that fails I give a short burst of misinformation to mislead and confuse. By this point he has reached mental collapse. Then, as a wise man once said, 'Kill one, scare one thousand.' Even the strong and strong-minded can fall victim, as they can't realise it is happening to them. They can't separate the mind game from the reality. The Psychology of Fear.

A great sadness to me is that I have never had any children of my own, although, over the years, I could have had a schoolyard full. I have lived with the harsh rule that a professional criminal should never have children as children can be weapons that one day can be used against you. An enemy with a wife and children ceases to be an enemy when the rules of true war are explained to him.

I have never, nor would I ever harm a child. The thought is repugnant. However, a father in a wheelchair cannot properly provide for children and as for a wife, 'It is too high up to eat grass' and she will soon leave him.

These rules, once explained, tend to dampen the passions for battle in the hearts of enemies. There are some animals in the criminal world who would sell their wife on the streets to buy bullets and teach their kids to steal so Dad can drink the money. Ridding a family of such a man is, to my mind, an act of charity.

Let me clarify the term 'street fighting'. I win because I am treacherous. If people want fair play, let them join a cricket club. A street fight is a no-holds-barred, anything-goes battle between two men or ten men. Anything can be used, from a slap on the face with a wet tea towel to a meat axe through the brain. Mainly fists, feet, knees, elbows and head butts are used, if a heavy object is not close to hand.

Personally, I would rather shoot someone than go through the messy business of fighting them. But in jail it is anything from bare fists to razor blades, butcher's knives to iron bars. To stand on top of the heap for 20 years simply means you are less frightened of death than the other fellow.

I don't fight to win, I fight to kill, so even if I don't kill I win. No crim could survive the baggings I've got. The only reason that I am still around is that I can fight like a death adder. But I know my limitations, I know that after 20 years I am not as strong or as big as I once was.

My old injuries play up. I suffer from short-term memory loss, a broken bone in my right hand which mended by itself gives me hell in the cold weather, my left shoulder aches in winter from the old ice-pick wound to the back of the neck and a bullet in the lower shoulder. I know that it is time to retire before someone retires me permanently.

Gambling and prostitution have always been the stock standard main players in the criminal world, but drugs have taken over the whole criminal culture. Prostitution is now legal in a manner of speaking, so drug money can be invested in parlours, brothels and escort agencies. Gambling is now an accepted illegal cover for criminals trying to conceal their true source of wealth. For example, 'I am not a drug dealer, I run a gambling club.' The fine for running an illegal gambling club is hardly worth mentioning.

It seems that every aspect of crime is geared around drugs, violence over drugs, females entering prostitution to pay for drugs, robberies committed to pay for drugs. In fact, I can't think of any area of crime that is not related to drugs in some way. Even standover men and torturers now stand over people connected with the drug world.

To call what's going on a drug problem is like calling AIDS a health problem or nuclear war an environmental problem. The drug culture has totally destroyed the criminal world and in my view will, in time, destroy normal society. Using coke, crack, smack, speed and smoking dope is now viewed by a large section of normal society as acceptable. In the case of the dreaded heroin, anti-drug preachers are seen as highly boring yawns.

In a matter of ten years children have turned into a flock of diehard environmentally aware and concerned young people, eager to fight the good fight for clean air and against toxic waste. Meanwhile, a great many of these same environmentally aware and concerned young people partake of assorted drugs, ignoring their own personal toxic intake.

Why was the education programme in relation to environmental issues put in front of anti-drugs education? The drug culture can only die in the classroom. Australia was once a nation of racists until the issue was fought in the classrooms, just as people have become rock solid environmentalists after the issue was fought in the schools.

However, the war against drugs has not been fought in the

schools. The government fires a few shots now and again, but no real war has ever truly been mounted. Maybe it is easier to fight non-profit issues, whereas drugs is a high-profit issue ... too much profit for too many people, I suspect. And in the end no one fights profit. That's my opinion.

Chapter 12

Sammy's Fatal Mistake

'I had nothing against him personally, but he made his move and lost.'

On November 24, 1986 Mark Brandon Read was released from Bendigo Prison after serving about nine years for attempting to kidnap Judge Martin from the County Court. During his time inside he was involved in a jail war which nearly cost him his life. In the decade in jail he had watched from the inside as certain underworld figures amassed fortunes. They were the sacred cows of the crime world, and had never been milked. The drug, gambling and vice industries were pumping out cash at an unprecedented rate, and Read wanted a piece of it. The violence inside had been for fun; now on the outside, he could do it for profit.

Not content just to be known as a hard crim, he wanted to be the biggest standover man in Australia. He flew to Tasmania with a plan, a plan to declare war on the major criminal crews of Melbourne. He had a place in Collingwood, and made flying sorties to Melbourne from Tasmania to shoot, bash and extort anyone he felt like standing over. He concentrated on drug dealers in the western suburbs, card games, gambling houses in Lygon Street, massage parlours and some respectable nightclubs. A favourite trick was to walk into a crowded disco with a stick of gelignite in his mouth and threaten to light it. This would tend to make people concentrate on the issues at hand, such as how much cash was to change hands. 'It's no use keeping it in your pocket where they can't see it,' Read once remarked of his penchant for gelignite.

The criminals of Melbourne were not going to allow one loose cannon to destroy empires that had taken decades to build. The word was soon out that Chopper was a walking dead man. Several contracts were taken out on him, including one for $50,000. 'The man who killed me would never have had to pay for a beer for the rest of his life, he would have been a hero,' Read noted later. One night in Collingwood four shots were fired at him. All missed — narrowly.

While this was going on he had contacted police through a prison officer and offered his services to a team of armed robbery squad detectives, headed by Rod Porter. Police hoped that Read could be turned to become a vital informer on the underworld heavyweights. He was given the police code name of Melville and detectives hoped he would provide information which would result in several major crimes being solved, particularly a $55,000 armed robbery in Glen Waverley where two guards were shot with machine guns.

Police received information of yet another contract on Read's life and advised him that things were too hot for him in Melbourne, and that he should return to Tasmania for a while. But Read ignored the advice. It would mean missing out on all the 'fun'.

On June 11, 1987, at the Fawkner Club Hotel in South Yarra, Read told police that while he was prepared to continue gathering information he wanted some extra 'insurance'. Rod Porter thought he wanted a gun, but Read said he just wanted a bullet-proof vest. That night in a park near the St Kilda Road police station Read was fitted with a bullet-proof vest provided by the detectives.

Several hours later, around 6.30 a.m., Read shot and killed a drug dealer, Siam Ozerkam, also known as Sammy the Turk, outside the Bojangles nightclub in St Kilda. Next day he lightheartedly told Porter that he committed the killing — but the armed robbery detectives thought his confession was a black joke. They felt he was testing them to see if they would relay the 'admission' to the homicide squad. In fact, they did tell homicide detectives in passing but, at that point, the investigators had another suspect in mind.

Read was later charged with the murder. Police alleged that while wearing the bullet-proof vest he shot and robbed Ozerkam. Read told the court that he was set up to be killed in the car park of Bojangles and killed Ozerkam in self-defence. He was acquitted but sentenced to five years jail for some of the many other offences he had committed during his crime rampage. He was charged and convicted for burning down the house of drug dealer, Nick Apostolidis, shooting Chris Liapis and firing shots into Apostolidis' mother's house.

He was out of jail for only seven months.

When he went back inside many heavyweight criminals felt safe again ... at least, for the time being.

It was a busy few months when I got out, there's no doubt about that, but you know what they say about busy hands. I made a bit of money when I was out but I had a few expenses too. It wasn't that cheap flying in and out from Tassie, I can tell you.

I have my version of events with silly Sam the Turk. The police have theirs. Obviously the jury believed me, God bless them. I have always had the greatest faith in the British Justice System and the common sense of the average person. But, I digress.

I went that night to Bojangles for a quiet drink, wearing a police bullet-proof vest and carrying a handgun down the front of my strides and a sawn-off .410 shotgun down the back. Anyone who has been to Bojangles will know that if anything I was a bit light on for fire power, when you consider the class of clientele that got there in the early hours of the morning.

There is no doubt that the Turk was set up to lure me outside, where I was going to be the victim of some serious mischief. This Turk tried to con me to go outside. He said he was going to sell me some guns.

He said, 'Come outside, we talk, ssh ssh, guns guns, business business.'

They've told this Turk to get Chopper out into the car park. The trouble is that Bojangles has two car parks. This knucklehead took me to the wrong car park. The rest of the gang were waiting for me in the front car park.

This Turk thought, no one's going to kill someone at the

front car park so they must mean the side car park. They were waiting out the front but we whizzed out to the side. A bad move. A fatal move, as it turned out, for Sammy.

He's turned around and looked at me and said, 'They'll be here in a minute.'

I thought, 'You shifty bastard.'

He said, 'You got gun, you got gun,' and I said, 'Yeah, I've got a gun,' and he asked where it was. I showed it to him. It was stuffed down the front of my pants. When he saw it he grabbed it and put it to my head. He wanted to blow my head right off. He thinks I'm a dickhead. The gun was an automatic. No one just picks up an automatic and fires it. You have to cock it.

He's got the gun at my head going click, click. The cheeky bastard had my gun out at my head going click, click, click.

But I carry two guns. I had the shotty down the back. I had a bullet-proof vest on, a sawn-off .410 shotgun down the back and the .32 at the front.

So I've pulled the shotty out and gone bang and it's bye bye Turk.

One hundred per cent genuine self-defence.
It had been 6.30 in the morning when Sammy had come up to me. He was part of a team with Frank Valastro and Graeme Jensen, both enemies of mine who were later to die at the hands of the police. They were with Shane Goodfellow that morning at Bojangles.

They claimed they wanted to talk to me to persuade me to

go back to Tasmania. In the car park at bloody Bojangles at 6.30 in the morning. Just to have a quiet word with me, you understand.

That lot wanted me dead and Sammy was the dummy they picked to set me up. But it all went wrong. The Turk made a stupid mistake by grabbing my gun ... and I blew his brains out through his left eye ball.

I had nothing against him personally, but he made his move and lost. In the chess game of life and death, you only get one move. His mates left him and ran. He was a stooge, used to get me outside. And when he did, they left him. It was a top stupid set-up, and if the crew outside had had the courage of their convictions – and any real guts – I'd be dead now.

I was found not guilty on the grounds of self-defence. I can't be tried twice for the same offence. Was it murder? No. It was clear-cut self-defence. However, from the moment he approached me I knew it was a set-up. As we walked outside I was ready. It was so childish and stupid. I marvelled at the thinking that went into such a childish and slap-happy plot. They were trying to kill a tiger snake with a feather duster.

Morally, maybe, it was murder. I could have shot him in both kneecaps and finished a game of cards before the would-be murder crew got their act together. But he had my own gun at my head. The fact that this poor simple mental retard couldn't make it work is beside the point. He tried to kill me – a stupidly inept attempt, but there can be no second chances. No one's ever given me a second chance.

Yes, poor Sammy was just a silly kid, a young up and comer. The weak mice who stooged him into it were the men who really murdered him. At the trial and in the newspapers it was alleged I was a police informer. Well, I deny that. I am not a police informer. There is no way known that I would be able to live in jail with some of the most dangerous men in Australia if any of them believed I was. I know police have publicly branded me an informer, but in my view that is really nothing but an attempt to commit murder by proxy. The fact is, no one has ever done a day's jail because of me.

I am not soliciting for donations, running for public office, nor am I the director of a multi-national corporation. I am not the host of a TV game show relying on popularity for ratings. Keeping those facts in mind, how is calling me names like 'informer' going to hurt me. I have never based my life on popularity and if name-calling and public condemnation is a strategic tactic employed to destroy me, then those who dreamt it up will have to think again.

But, anyway, that is all in the past now. It is doubtful that I will be invited to any more drinking sessions at the Fawkner Club. I am alive and well and acquitted of murder. The police involved have moved on to other duties out of harm's way – and far away from Chopper Read. As long as I have no bullets coming at me through the taxi window as I go to the airport I'm quite happy to leave this old bone well and truly buried. I will probably never really know just what the hell I was really walking into that dark morning at Bojangles. Or who really pulled the strings that jerked the puppets.

SAMMY THE TURK

She said get The Chopper out of the bar,
Shane and the boys are in the car,
If you can help set up the Big Fella, Turk, you'll be a star,
The boys farmed it out, they got it ghosted,
But as Sammy walked out the door, the boys just left him posted.
The game was for real, it was no lark,
But Sammy walked toward the wrong car park,
Silly boys, was all The Chopper had to say,
It wasn't their lucky day,
And poor Sammy the Turk got blown away.

Chapter 13

God Bless Juries

*'If I could fix a race horse as quick and easily as a Crown
witness I'd be a millionaire.'*

The court system in Australia is not what it
seems. By that I don't mean it's corrupt in the
way of cash corruption. The Americans and
South Americans may have to pay a fortune to get what
we get free here under the 'Old Mates Act'.

Australia has the old school tie in reverse syndrome.
Justice Lionel Murphy summed up the Australian legal
system here in just five words: 'What about my little
mate?'

As for fixing a trial. If I could fix a race horse as quick
and easily as a Crown witness then I'd be a millionaire.

All it needs is for a non-threatening person to approach the Crown witness – a man of the cloth of any
denomination is my favourite – and simply say: 'Look,
no one is dirty on you. We all understand the situation
you're in. It's all sweet now, you can pull out of this.'

The message is simple. Come home, all is forgiven;

that sort of thing.

If the witness can't do that, then it is taken one step further: 'Look, give your evidence but screw it up. Make 100 mistakes, forget things. That way you have kept your bargain with the police and the Crown and no one is dirty on you. The accused walks, no blue, no problem, all is well. Just screw up your evidence.'

A 'got-at' Crown witness is actually better than no Crown witness at all. The worst Crown witness is a truly frightened one or a really angry one.

Sweetening a Crown witness is a bloody must in my book. Everyone has a wife, a mother, a sister or a girlfriend. They get the message: give your evidence, but screw the guts out of it and everything will be sweet. No big deal; it goes on all the time.

Any Crown witness taken from the criminal world is a liar anyway, so getting him to tell a few lies for the defence as well as the prosecution is like falling off a log.

The game of let's make a deal is played in every courthouse in Australia, always has been and always will be. Maybe a little cash is handed to the lawyer to encourage him to get in there and see what he can do but the system is based on 'Can we do a deal, can we make this go away?'

Near enough is good enough ... the easy way out ... what about my little mate ... he's one of us ... he's on our side, he's a good bloke, he's given us a lot of help ... he plays footy for this team or that team ... his dad's a policeman ...

he's in the right Lodge ... he's willing to nod to this if we drop that ... any chance of a fine, how about a bond?

Nudge nudge, wink wink. The legal system is a never-ending round of let's make a deal.

It is not corrupt, but it's the next best thing and doesn't have to cost the player a penny. It is a purely Australian thing.

Some of these assorted deals are actually struck at the very door of the court itself. Because no cash changes hands the people playing the game think it is OK. The Australian court room is an old whore and she doesn't get a penny for her trouble.

It's the Australian way.

I should thank my legal team who got me out of my murder trial: solicitor Mr Pat Harvey, barrister Mr Boris Kayser and Queen's Counsel, Mr Colin Lovitt. It was their sterling legal work which helped me beat the charge.

However, God helps those who help themselves and I did walk into the court room with a slight edge. I can now say that I had the assistance of a very 'confused' Crown witness. Plus I was a hated man, who most of the criminal world dreamed of killing, and I was pleading self-defence. How could I lose?

They tried to kill me and when that failed they tried to get me life. The fact that I was carrying two guns and wearing a bullet-proof vest when Sammy the Turk got his and the

Crown had a witness who saw the whole thing, swearing that it was cold-blooded murder, didn't seem to bother the jury, God bless them.

Some of the witnesses were criminals, self-confessed drug users and prostitutes. It didn't sit too well with the jury. If they had sold tickets to the trial they could have made a lot of money.

It was really a set-up to kill me and it was genuinely self-defence, but how I beat it has still got me puzzled.

One of the witnesses was the former de facto of the drug dealer, Nick the Greek, and he advised her to give evidence. He was named in the court by the Crown as one of the four men who put money up to have a contract taken out on me. Personally I don't think those nitwits did put a contract out on me. They wouldn't know how to do it and they wouldn't have the guts. The Crown witnesses were frantic to have me put away for life. I'm sure their evidence convinced the jury of my innocence.

I have known for many years that if you fill a court room with enough bullshit then the truth can walk in and out of the dock without ever being seen.

There are several big cases where this has been done, but it is a very dangerous game for fools to play.

Never think that the courtroom is the place where the truth is found.

Forgive me. I shouldn't gloat over such matters.

The reason most guilty men walk free is because poor old

mum and dad juries simply find the evidence impossible to believe. That is why crime and the profits from crime is becoming a billion-dollar growth industry.

Simply put, Mr and Mrs average Aussie don't really believe it is all happening here. They think it is too far-fetched and only happens in America or Colombia or in the movies. Let me tell you it is happening here, madder and crazier than even I could describe.

The Australian criminal world is a totally unbelievable, blood-soaked, insane, comedy of errors. It is filled with the most unrealistic, nuttiest collection of murdering, drug-running, movie-watching Walter Mittys you will ever find.

By comparison, I think my story is quite a simple one. Some people think of things in terms of black and white, right and wrong, good and evil. But the real world is made with shades of grey. That is the world where all men have to walk, especially those in the criminal world.

For example, in 1977, I had to meet a group of men at the Morning Star Hotel in Prahran in relation to a matter concerning Billy Longley. They were police officers, with the standover figure Brian Kane acting as some sort of middle man.

Kane patted me down. I had a sawn-off shotgun on me, but I was only patted down for a wire or listening device. The shotgun was allowed. In short, the police were very concerned about rumours and stories that I was about to launch forth a revenge war against some of the dockers on behalf of Billy. They were concerned that innocent people could be hurt in the crossfire.

They were trying to stop a war before it started because they did not want another bout of bloodshed. These police were honest men. However, in the name of the greater common good they were prepared to turn a blind eye to outstanding matters in relation to myself. They even understood my need to carry a gun. Kane was also armed at the time.

What the police were doing was trying to stop a bloodbath before it happened and, therefore, save innocent lives. But if that meeting in the back bar of that pub had been discovered, the police would have had no option but to claim that Brian Kane and Chopper Read were informers so they could cover themselves, as the truth of the meeting could hardly be revealed.

Police are not legally empowered to call warring underworld factions together for shifty, under-the-counter peace deals. But, regardless of that fact, meetings and secret arrangements which can save lives on both sides of the fence were and are made all the time.

There are grey areas where police and criminals are forced to walk now and again in the common interest. Sometimes there can be a common enemy or a common interest, such as when a small child is raped or kidnapped. That is when all previous bad blood can be put aside for the common good. These deals will never be admitted in a million years but nothing is ever black and white.

There are all sorts of under-the-counter meetings between police and criminals. The crims are not necessarily acting as informers and the police are not taking bribes. However, neither side would like these meetings, deals, or arrangements to be made public. The problem, from the official point of view, is that the only legal reason that a policeman has to meet a criminal, other than to arrest him, is if the crim is an informer.

The modern police force discourages the secret meetings that have been held in the past. If meetings had been called early in the game then Walsh Street and Russell Street could have been avoided.

The under-the-counter secret arrangement saved many lives in the 1920s, 30s, 40s, 50s, 60s and 70s. The oldtimers can tell of peace meetings between different warring factions that have involved the police.

The biggest one I can remember being told about was after the murder of Freddie 'The Frog' Harrison. The entire back room of a Port Melbourne Hotel was locked off with drinks and light eats provided.

The Dockies used to put barrels on for the talks. The Press was never invited and the Chief Commissioner would not be welcome. It was held on neutral ground at one time about once a month. Even an escaped convict could walk in and walk out and not be arrested. The idea was to sort out any shit before it cost lives. The only reason that I didn't put about 20 gallons of petrol into Lygon Street after shots were fired at me in 1987 was because of an under-the-counter meeting which sorted it out.

I have never heard of a crim refusing to attend one of the meetings.

The police no longer call these under-the-counter back-bar meetings. Meanwhile the death toll mounts up.

It is my firm opinion every main player in the Australian underworld has to have some form of a relationship with certain key people within the police forces. If that relationship is caught out then the police can only offer the excuse that the criminal is an informer. This is not always the case. And the police involved are not always corrupt, either.

The game of cops and robbers is a strange one; I understand even the KGB and the CIA meet now and again to clear up certain unresolved matters, and it's like that in law enforcement.

When I was last out of jail I had a relationship with certain members of the Armed Robbery Squad. The police concerned were Rod 'Rocket' Porter, Steve 'Dirty Larry' Curnow, Bryan (whose nickname is too foul to quote) Cook, and Barry 'The Boy' Hahnel, who later went to jail himself.

I will sum this relationship up by saying that the enemy of my enemy is my friend and I feel they shared the same view. In the court they had their version of events and I had mine, but as both sides know the truth and court rooms don't always mix.

I must say now that all the dust has settled and all the mud has been thrown, that I hold no personal ill-will towards any of them. I would like to remind them, however, of our first conversation, 'When you shake hands with the devil, you can't complain about a little blood on the footpath'.

I always found Rocket Rod Porter to be a good bloke. He never took drugs in his life but when he was in my company he used to get a little worried. It may have been that I liked to tease him. I said to him once, 'I don't know what you are on, but if we had a pound of it we could make a fortune.'

When we were in a pub I would talk in a really loud voice and he would look around and say, 'Keep your voice down, you mad bugger'.

I nicknamed him 'clockwork orange' because he was easy to wind up and he would turn red when he got embarrassed. When they fitted me out with the bullet-proof vest after a good session at the Fawkner Club Hotel it was a total comedy. It was in a little park behind the St Kilda Road police complex about 10.20 at night. A few hours later Sammy the Turk was no more.

They later denied any knowledge of me carrying a gun. For Christ's sake, I wouldn't meet my dear old mother without a gun.

A lot of know-all crims who decide to rabbit on about things they really don't know about come out with the old line about corruption and big cash bribes. Basically it is pure bullshit; they've been watching too much American TV.

I've met a hell of a lot of police in Melbourne who I would describe as 'open-minded' and 'liberated thinkers' when it came to inter-criminal violence and bloodshed. They didn't mind turning a blind eye and a deaf ear to 'poetic justice' and the common good, but as far as bribery is concerned, the only crims I know who claim to have bribed police with big money are all serving long jail terms. You figure it out.

It does go on, but it comes undone just as quickly. It is an area only fools enter into and is not popular in Melbourne. The handshake over a few beers and a personal arrangement between the two sides to work out a problem under the counter is the way most things are done. Cash bribes are just too damn risky, stupid and dangerous. The bribe is not trusted in Melbourne. Almost every idiot that gets involved in cash corruption comes undone because the Aussie has never trusted it. It is not the Aussie way.

As far as bribe-taking police are concerned, I wish they were listed in the Yellow Pages, because I'm buggered if I was able to find any of them when I wanted them. The only time I ever offered a bribe to a copper to fix a problem was in 1987, when I offered $20,000 – and got a knock-back.

People are more interested in finding out the easiest way to solve a problem than making money from corruption. With corruption comes paranoia: people fear they will be betrayed and they lose trust. Then the deal collapses with someone spilling their guts.

When you meet with police, if you were to offer them money they would say, 'Hang on, we're not bent.' If the police offered the crims money they would say, 'We're not working for you.'

The only time money raised its ugly head when I was involved with the Armed Robbery Squad was when Rocket Rod Porter and I had to work out whose shout it was at the bar.

Sometimes the sides can get together to screw the umpire and a cent never changes hands.

I think the police in Melbourne are more enthusiastic over blood and guts than the ones in Sydney. But the NSW coppers are far quicker to put their hands out for a sling.

In Melbourne we have the shifty deal. I think it is more honest.

THE SHIFTY DEAL

The Australian Courts don't hold no grudge,
A nod's as good as a wink,
To a blind Judge,
No need for cash, the brief's been paid,
All praise the name of Legal Aid,
The Crown is hoping for an early night,
No need to struggle,
No need to fight,

'Look, boys, I'll drop this,
You plead to that,'
And all home in time,
To feed the cat,
No cash needed here,
Nor money down,
Forget the Yanks,
This is Melbourne Town,
'I'll do this for you,
You do that for me,
We can sort this out,
Just wait and see,'
The courts, crooks and coppers all know the feel,
Of the classic Aussie shifty deal.

Chapter 14

The Plastic Godfathers

'Freddy is a thickset, broad-shouldered, barrel-chested man with the physical strength of a small bull — and the courage of a rice bubble.'

There are certain criminals who get around Melbourne with big reputations thinking they are the mafia. Most of them are jokes. They bore me to tears. Their idea of mafia is to wear dark glasses in Lygon Street.

If you stand on a corner in Lygon Street wearing dark glasses and slip-on shoes and there's more than two of you, then you're in the mafia. It's just ridiculous. These plastic crims, with their car phones and coke habits, they try to follow anything on American television. They aren't tough at all.

There is one silly fat fool I've known for years, and as long as there's a crim to sell down the drain neither he nor any of that Canton Crew will do a day's jail.

It is well known in criminal circles that there are four main police stations in Melbourne: St Kilda Road,

Russell Street, William Street ... and Lygon Street. More crims have been given up by that lot of would-be pretenders than in the rest of Melbourne. So much for the mafia code of silence. They wouldn't know anything about it. If that fat Plastic Godfather ever ended up in here he would get a welcome he would never forget.

You are dealing with crims today who 'fought' their way through the back streets of 'tough' suburbs like Lower Templestowe, North Balwyn and East Ivanhoe. I was brought up in Thomastown. We thought the people in West Heidelberg were posh because they had sewerage.

The crims today come from quite affluent backgrounds. It's shocking when you think about it. There is no excuse for some of them being inside. Some of them have matriculated, some have been to university. It's drugs that have got them here, you understand.

It's not the same any more. I don't want to spend the rest of my life mixing with this lot. Honestly, there are crims in here in their 20s who talk about the *Teenage Mutant Ninja Turtles*. How can you spend your time with people like that?

The hard crims were the men with the dash to fight each other in the field of combat; they were the ones respected in the underworld. But now it is the man with drug connections. Some weak insipid, effeminate, little character calls the shots.

The number of crims who have *Scarface* on video at home is ridiculous. The Carlton Crew all have *Godfather One, Two* and *Three* on video. They have been talking about taking a contract out on me: $15,000 down and $15,000 when the job is completed. These so-called contracts are generally made in loud voices and in public, at card games or late at night at nightclubs.

The aim is to impress the crowd and to frighten me. All I can do is pass on the words of an old mentor and one of the world's really hard men: 'If the mafia is so tough, why don't they have a branch office in Belfast?' The bad blood between me and the Carlton Crew is a thing of the past as far as I am concerned. They can keep their paranoid ways. I know that some criminals have been trying to play both sides off against each other for well over four years.

It has been a classic case of the mice trying to manipulate the lions. We will never all walk down Lygon Street hand in hand but the days of blood feuding are over. Simply because I am walking away. As for the plastic gangsters, they wouldn't know how close they came to learning first hand what real blood and guts underworld warfare was like, on the receiving end. If things had turned out a little differently in 1987 quite a few of them might have been caught in Operation Wog Fry, the plan I had to torch Lygon Street with petrol.

To give you an example of some of the nitwits who are supposed to be 'crime bosses' I will give you a profile on one of the men who is supposed to be a Godfather.

I have always known him as 'Freddy the Wog'. He is a

thickset, broad-shouldered, barrel-chested man, with the physical strength of a small bull and the courage of a rice bubble. He is connected in illegal gambling, speed factories, massage parlours and escort services. He has a fearful reputation as a man who will put a contract out on anyone if they cross him. But in my humble opinion, he couldn't organise a hit on his next door neighbour's cat.

He started off as a street fighter in Brunswick and got a reputation as a tough man, gunfighter, standover man and nightclub gangster around Melbourne in the late 1960s and early '70s. He made that reputation with violence against females, taking their money and beating harmless drunks half to death. He would never appear in pubs and clubs without a small army of two-bob tough guys and hangers-on to back him up. With a gun he was a razzle dazzle boy, pistol-whipping drunks and weak people, pulling out the gun to impress the ladies. In the early days he only had a replica; it wasn't until later that he actually owned a real one.

Freddy's right-hand men were a half-crazy Albanian named Machine Gun Charlie who, in truth, never owned a machine gun, and Frankie Long Nose, a two-bob mafia pretender. Freddy's hero was the American gangster, Al Capone, and Freddy loved people to call him 'Mr Capone'. Freddy was another one of these nitwits who read every gangster and mafia book ever written and tried to live in a mafia fantasy land, later encouraging his younger brothers to do the same. I punched on twice with Freddy, once at the

Hard Rock Cafe and the other time at Johnny's Green Room. Let me tell you, for all his giant reputation, I have met school girls who could beat him in a fight. In the world of really hard men his name and those of his brothers don't rate a mention.

I once stuffed this idiot head-first into a large litter bin outside a Melbourne nightclub. He was a pansy then and money hasn't improved him He has got into drugs now and is one of the biggest names in the heroin industry. He is hero-worshipped by a large number of young Italian criminals, and involved with criminal crews in several states. The Carlton Crew in Melbourne is but one. Yet he prefers to live interstate for safety reasons. He may be rich now, but to me he is still just another limp-wristed pansy gangster.

Freddy is the prime example of how money and drugs can turn a mouse into a monster. Personally I would like to have grabbed Freddy, kidnapped him and introduced him to the old blowtorch. However, he became wealthy while I was in jail during the early 1980s, and he was living out of the state when I got out. Why he hasn't gone on the missing list already is a mystery to me. He is very smart, but I have never met a coward who didn't have his fair share of rat cunning. Meanwhile Freddy has the money to live out his Al Capone fantasy. Walter Mitty spends a lot of time at Freddy's house, believe me.

A lot of men in jail are there because of Freddy. But, although he's such a big operator, he's not in jail. The truth is

Freddy has been the target for assorted police forces for ten years but he has survived the way most of them do. What he does is 'create' other drug lords for the police to grab. Freddy will provide top-grade smack for up and comers, then remove himself and work through a middle man. The up and comers may start with a simple bag of smack, 28 grams or so. They cut the stuff six times and make their money. They get bigger and bigger until they too are major dealers. Each may sell a pound a week, all supplied through Freddy's middle men. They then become police targets and can be given up before anyone gets too close to Freddy.

Freddy has made his money from them and these monkeys can be replaced. Many of them have only dealt through middle men and never know that Freddy is the power behind the scene. The police are happy because they have grabbed what they believe are one or two major dealers, and that takes the heat off Freddy. Some multi-million-dollar drug bosses arrested, charged and convicted were Freddy's monkeys and they didn't even know it.

The term for this is the 'swap out'. When the police get close to Freddy he gives them the swap out; it has kept him out of jail for years. Two major drug dealers are in Pentridge now because of a swap out. They were given up by a middle man who takes his orders from Freddy.

Freddy the Wog is really a self-made man. He gave himself the nickname, earned a reputation for violence based on nothing, and created an image for himself. He has risen to become one of the most powerful and feared drug lords in Australia, but in truth he is nothing but a paper tiger. He remains afloat by getting rid of his enemies by setting them up with the police. He is a skilled man at surviving by treachery.

Another major figure we will call Al is Lygon Street's answer to Robert De Niro. He goes under many names: The Fairy Godfather, The Plastic Gangster, Melbourne's Princess of Crime, the King of Paranoia and the Italian French Poodle. That's right, I don't like Al. I first met him when he was 19, pinching money out of girls' handbags in nightclubs while the chicks were on the dance floor.

I've never heard of Al having a punch on without having 10 or 12 helpers backing him up. He is a bully and he picks his mark. He will only fight if he can win. He started off as a bouncer at the two-up school; he has shot a few drunks in the leg at nightclubs and he has learnt how to run card games. He may be rich and he may be well-connected but the hole he will one day go into has already been dug.

He lives in fear, a prisoner of his own wealth. He is backed up by a private army of kick boxers, gunmen and bouncers, all with their hands out for money. The only one in that crew with guts and brains is the one called Mick, who has the sense not to shoot his mouth off.

Every time Al needs some advice he puts on *The Godfather* movie to see how Marlon Brando did it. Once I went to say a friendly hello to him in a card game in Lygon Street – with a stick of gelignite. Funny thing, Al wouldn't come out of the toilets for a chat.

This big clown may be a hero to a large part of the criminal world but personally I wouldn't give him a job as a towel boy in a gay Turkish bath; he wouldn't be tough enough. He is another of that crew who is the master of the swap-out, which is why he hasn't been to jail.

Once I would have liked a full-on war with this crew, but now I couldn't care less. But if any of them try coming to Tasmania to look for me they'd better get one-way tickets, because they won't be coming back.

One of the longest reigning and luckiest criminals in Melbourne would have to be the drug dealer known as The Tiger. I first met him when I was 16 in the Turana boys' home when I did four months. The Tiger has come a long way since then and would now be a millionaire, owning houses and land in Newport, Williamstown and the south eastern suburbs. He buys houses and land like other men buy socks.

Tiger owns property in Lygon Street and is a financial partner in some of the illegal gambling haunts in that area. He is another member of the Canton Crew. He relies on some of them for protection. He keeps large amounts of money in trust accounts held by certain suspect solicitors. He gambles heavily and likes to call himself a professional punter. He also breeds and fights American pit bull terriers and considers that good sport. He cuts the ears off all his dogs to give them that mean, clean-cut look.

Tiger has a large collection of jewellery and has given me a solid gold ring with 32 diamonds in it. I never had to put The Tiger in the boot; he would toss money at me whenever he saw me. I once took a .32 revolver, put a slug in it, spun it, closed it, put it to my head and pulled the trigger – 'click'. Then I put it to The Tiger's head – 'click' again. He nearly fainted. I did, however, shoot one of his bodyguards once. That chap decided when he recovered that it would be in his best interests to resettle overseas – a wise move in these troubled times.

The Tiger had money everywhere. I once walked into his home and found $5,000 in cash lying beside an electric heater. He had plenty and there was no need to torture him. He was physically weak. I was once offered $5,000 to shoot him but I refused. He was paranoid, having more bodyguards than the Queen of England.

Why would I want to kill him when he was my own Golden Goose? I could get money out of The Tiger with just a phone call. He always carried between $5,000 and $10,000 in $100 bills for spending money. He would give me $1,000 or $2,000 every time I would say hello to him, which is what I call good manners. He would also pinpoint other drug dealers for me to grab.

He once took me to the footy to see Footscray play the

Sydney Swans. We were both a little pissed and standing near the fence. Naturally I was well armed even though it was just a day out. The Tiger pointed out Warwick Capper, who was on the field and only 30 feet away. The Tiger said, 'Chopper, put a bullet though that bastard's kneecap and you can name your own price.' He was quite serious in his suggestion, but I just laughed it off. If I had been a little drunker at the time, who knows what could have happened?

The Tiger stays afloat by swapping out his monkeys, the people who deal drugs with him. This is a trick which was taught to him by his idol, Freddy the Wog. The Tiger has invested his money so well that the drug world is just a hobby to him. He has never been to jail. However, a great many people who have blame the experience on being swapped out by The Tiger.

He once put up a great amount of money to have me killed and the men who accepted the contract went straight to the race track and lost it. He once sat at his kitchen table with 60 grand in front of him and burst into tears because he could not get anyone to kill me. He may be an evil bastard, but he has his funny side and, in one way, I kind of liked him.

Tiger is the king of smack in the western suburbs and while he is not a fighter or a gunman he is still dangerous. He is one of the most protected drug bosses in Australia. He is not a smartarse gangster. He tries very hard to be low key and to keep a low profile. He is probably the worst-dressed and scruffiest-looking millionaire in Melbourne. I used to tell him he should use some of his money on plastic surgery and a face lift because he is dog ugly. He has a head like a robber's dog.

He prefers to spend his money on private detectives and electronic security. He keeps files on his enemies, his friends, other criminals and police. He has a collection of tape recordings which could start a Royal Commission. While I doubt that The Tiger will ever go to jail I believe it is only a matter of time before he is collected by some headhunter. Of all the drug lords The Tiger is the shiftiest I have met. He is the classic cunning coward.

Many of the Italian gangsters around town have big tickets on themselves. Those in the know will tell you they're not even the biggest ethnic group in the crime world. I was once told by a Sicilian criminal that there were two sorts of Italian crims — Sicilians and the rest — and he said that as long as I didn't mess with Sicilians I could do whatever I liked to the rest. I said: 'Sure, Tony' ... then I shot him.

THE FAIRY GANGSTERS

If the mafia had a comedy,
Then Melbourne's the song they'd sing,
Led by a buttercup Vito,
Who likes to be the King,
He looks like a million dollars,
In slip-on shoes and shirt,

And rumour has it, after hours, he slips on a lady's skirt,
He carries a gun, just for fun, and keeps money in his shoe,
So if you're hunting for his wallet, I think the rumour's true,
And with his gang of hangers-on, they look a funny sight,
They love to bag The Chopper, every day and night,
They get down to the two-up, where they love to stand and meet,
The two-bob fairy gangsters,
The crew from Lygon Street.

Chapter 15

The Walsh Street Cowards

'Walsh Street was a shitpot murder. It was without honour or courage.'

On October 12, 1988, two young policemen, Steven Tynan and Damian Fyre, were on routine night patrol when they received a call to go to Walsh Street, South Yarra, to check reports that a white Holden sedan had been abandoned in the middle of the road.

The inexperienced pair had been set up – lured to their deaths by a gang of men who gunned them down in the street. Police believe the two constables were killed in revenge for the death at police hands of Graeme Jensen only hours earlier.

Jensen, a convicted bandit, was shot dead by police outside a Narre Warren shopping centre the day before the Walsh Street murders by members of the armed robbery squad.

In 1987 another associate, Frank Valastro, had been shot dead by police in his East Bentleigh home as he was mixing cocaine and sugar. Police said he was armed with an automatic pistol when he was shot.

Police and the community were stunned by the Walsh Street killings. There were grave fears that a 'war' would erupt between sections of the underworld and the police.

A special police task force working on the Walsh Street shootings eventually concluded that the slaughter was carried out by members of an underworld family considered one of the most vicious in Australia — the Allen and Pettingill clan.

Some members of the family, headed by former prostitute and brothel-keeper Kathleen Pettingill, have been implicated in murder, armed robbery and drug matters.

Notorious members included Dennis Bruce Allen, a drug dealer, pimp, gunrunner, police informer and murderer who died of natural causes in April 1987.

Allen had a weekly drug turnover of nearly $100,000 in the mid-1980s, and was known as Mr Death. Chopper Read had bashed him in Pentridge years earlier and Allen vowed that no matter how long it took or how much money it cost, he would get Read killed.

When Allen died of heart disease he was waiting to stand trial over the murder of Wayne Patrick Stanhope.

Dennis Allen's brother, Peter John Allen, was the smartest of the brood. He was considered a man with a good grasp of the law, although it hasn't kept him out of jail.

Peter Allen is a convicted heroin dealer and former member of the top ten most-wanted list in Victoria.

At one stage he bragged on the telephone that he made between $30,000 and $35,000 a week He was able to buy a house in Templestowe and pay it off in three months. Eventually the courts stripped him of all his assets, although he argued he should be able to *keep Dennis's old bullet-proof vest for sentimental reasons.*

The Walsh Street task force eventually arrested Peter Allen's half brothers, Victor George Peirce and Trevor Pettingill. Also arrested were Anthony Leigh Farrell and Peter David McEvoy.

Another man alleged to have been involved in the Walsh Street murder plot, Jedd Houghton, was shot dead by police in a Bendigo caravan park on November 17, 1988.

The Crown alleged that the gang were friends of Jensen and decided to kill police at random as a payback for the death of their mate.

The prosecution claimed the gang had sworn a bizarre pact to kill 'two cops for one crim'.

One of the key witnesses was Jason John Ryan, the nephew of Peirce and Pettingill. After a controversial six-week trial, a Supreme Court Jury acquitted all four in March 1991, after six days of deliberation.

All those charged have maintained their innocence.

After being acquitted McEvoy and Peirce yelled that they believed they would be killed. At one point McEvoy said: 'I'm not afraid to die.'

Mark Brandon Read, no stranger to violence, gives his view on Walsh Street, and the men who were acquitted of the charge.

What better way to die than to face fearful odds, for the ashes of your family and the honour of your Gods.

That sums up my feelings towards revenge. Revenge to me

is a highly personal thing. Revenge is a dish best eaten cold, and it has no time limit.

No crim in Melbourne would dare speak of this topic; it is taboo. But I will. Walsh Street was a shitpot murder. It was without honour or courage.

Who did it is not the point. I couldn't give a shit. Graeme Jensen was an enemy of mine who ran like a little puppy and couldn't beat time with a bass drum, so his death didn't concern me at all. But if he had been my friend and I thought revenge was in order, I would have watched and waited, smiled and acted in a friendly and polite manner while gathering the correct information on exactly who killed him. And then I would have hunted the men responsible, even if it meant walking into the places where they worked.

I would have faced them in the light of day and gunned them down like dogs. Then I would have pleaded guilty with my head held proud, blood for blood, revenge with honour. You don't gun down babies in the dead of night and then run like dogs. That is not revenge. Revenge to me is a religion; it is a holy duty. If a friend dies, then the offender dies, blood for blood ... not blood for nothing.

Every man knows what it is like to be stirred by the emotion of revenge. True revenge, while not legally condoned, is totally understood.

Innocent men died and lives were destroyed as a result of Walsh Street, just because a bunch of would-be gangsters didn't have the guts to do the job right. If the men who had killed Jensen had been faced and killed in blood combat in the name of revenge, no cop in Melbourne would have called it cowardly.

A well-known criminal, Shane Goodfellow, gave evidence against me at my murder trial. Farrell and Pettingill and the one they call 'Bubble Brain' thought it was funny that he jumped the box against me. On the other hand Victor Peirce was heard to say that Goodfellow had done the wrong thing, but the other mice laughed.

They should remember that the friends of my enemy are also my enemies.

I first met Victor Peirce when he was 14 years old in 1974. Some would-be tough guys wouldn't let him into the Graham Hotel in the city and I corrected their manners. At the time I was friendly with his brother, Peter 'six shots rapid fire' Allen, a young gunman and criminal serving time in B Division.

Victor was a harmless sort of kid, he was about 14 and I was 19 or 20. I belted some bloke, hit him once in the head once and he fell and fell hard. He must have hit his head hard on the cement and the blood ran free. Poor little Victor had a look in his eye that was pure horror. I put my arm around young Victor and said, 'It's OK, Vic. You're with me.'

Years later he was in H Division with his mate 'Bubble Brain'. By then Victor was a big mover with a reputation and a power base of his own. But when he saw me he became that 14-year-old kid all over again.

Which goes to show that you can fool some of the people all of the time, and you can even fool all of the people some of the time, but in the world of blood and guts you don't fool Chopper Read any of the time.

As for 'Bubble Brain', if he has ever won a fight then I certainly haven't heard about it. The bald wimp used to drop his gangster facade real quick when he looked into my eyes. Ha ha.

He has a few rather nasty enemies in the criminal world as he has a reputation as a 'lash', a man who does not like to pay his debts, and a backdoor merchant who takes advantage of other men's wives and girlfriends.

If you mix a man with a big mouth and a gangster complex who couldn't punch his way through a lady's lace hanky, you end up with a coward who is eager to impress. He swaggers around and if it wasn't for his bubble-brain bald head he would try to act like Robert De Niro. He is quite a comedy and not well respected in the meaner circles of the criminal world. The Bubble has two brothers who are prison officers and this is a sore point with him. You wouldn't even call The Bubble a real crim.

The Bubble used to nearly wet his pants when he saw me. The facts are that a limp-wrist, two-bob pansy is a bum whether he beats a murder blue or wins a Brownlow medal. That lot are as heavy as feather dusters, Walsh Street or no Walsh Street.

In the world of hard men, blokes like Anthony Farrell and Trevor Pettingill don't even rate a mention. All I can say about Pettingill is that he is a runt junkie in a flashy suit his mummy bought him. As a heavy and a gunman and street fighter, I'd say an angry schoolgirl armed with a tennis racquet would give him a flogging without raising a sweat.

As for Farrell, I had to act as a bodyguard for Mad Charlie once in 1987. Charlie had to go to the Cricketers Arms Hotel in Cruickshank Street, Port Melbourne, to meet Anthony Farrell's dad, Tony Farrell, nicknamed 'Mushie' – an ex-pro boxer and petty crim – regarding a debt Charlie needed to collect.

Farrell paid up.

He was in the company of his young, pretty, baby-faced, blond-haired son, Anthony. He was there to add security for his father ... ha ha.

I laughed and said: 'Hey, Anthony, you'd be better off getting a dress and becoming a drag queen.' He was not amused and flounced out of the pub like a little girl in a huff. It was all very funny. Even his dad, Mushie, saw the joke, as Anthony is not, and never will be, what his dad was. Not that Mushie was any great fighter, but at least he has some fighting skill and guts.

To be honest, that crew and I mix on a different social level within the criminal world. Victor Peirce's OK. I've known him since he was a teenager and he's harmless enough. But the rest are a spoilt, petty, evil-minded bunch of girls. I didn't like Jensen. But I'll tell you this – Jensen didn't like Farrell or Pettingill, so what all the bullshit was about, I don't know.

The ridiculous thing with that joke crew is that after Walsh Street, most criminals will not be seen talking against them. It is as if being critical of them means that you are on the police side. But everyone misses the point: that crew was a pack of petty crooks and wimps before Walsh Street and they haven't climbed the social ladder since. They beat the murder blue, and so what.

I make no statement on who killed the two police in Walsh Street but if it was an act of revenge it failed. The police who killed Jensen are alive. What annoys me is that the joke crew have been elevated to heavy crims and that some crooks may give them respect they do not deserve.

The word was out after the acquittal that some members of this joke crew were going to get paid large amounts of cash by sections of the media to tell their stories. Alas, it turned out to be a false rumour. If they had made some wealth from it all they would have been spending it in wheelchairs as I know a few chaps who would have been quick to ask for a donation.

If I wasn't walking away and retiring I would probably put that crew of fools in the boot ... just for the fun of it. In 1979 I broke nearly every bone in Graeme Jensen's head. At the time he was considered to be one of the if not the best and most violent street fighter in Melbourne. I got him in the number two shower yard of H Division. He walked in a rooster and was carried out a feather duster. Jensen and his team of nitwits attacked me with iron bars in Bendigo jail in 1986. They attacked me like mad dogs – until I pulled out a tomahawk. Then they ran like French poodles.

Frankie Valastro was a psycho, a pint-sized Italian version of Squizzy Taylor. He would shoot the eyes out of your grandmother and rape her on the way down. I first met him in J Division in 1971. We were all having showers and I'm afraid that Valastro turned around to find the extra stream of warm water running down his back was Chopper relieving himself – all in the name of humour, you understand. I'm afraid the bad blood went on from there. He later hooked up with the Lygon Street crowd.

Valastro, Jensen and Shane Goodfellow were at Bojangles when I killed Sammy the Turk. There is no doubt they were waiting for me outside the nightclub that night. As for Sammy, I'd never met him. He must have been a friend of theirs.

The Melbourne underworld is a mass of shadows and dark tunnels. Some of the most cunning plots and plans the KGB and CIA have ever cooked up against each other would be considered commonplace in the Melbourne criminal world. It is a world of treachery, counter-treachery, betrayal and double agents.

The crews and gangs in Melbourne can often be inter-related. In fact, it's a world of criminal incest. Some females in that scene have been girlfriend, wife and de facto to six or seven different crooks belonging to different gangs and, as a result of the children born, members of warring gangs can find themselves 'related'.

For example, Sandra Faure was Keithy Faure's wife and Graeme Jensen's de facto and the two men were at war. One bloke had seven kids to five de factos, all sisters of crims. In Melbourne, the Allen family had kids to de facto wives, nearly all sisters of crims. A gang war can be a real 'family feud'.

Jensen back-doored Keithy Faure with Keithy's wife, Sandra. I am no great friend of Faure but that sort of thing shouldn't be done. It causes ill-feeling, and people get hurt.

In my opinion, the only member of the Allen–Pettingill– –Peirce clan with any guts and brains is Peter John Allen.

I've known Peter Allen about 20 years. He got the nickname 'Six Shots' after he and another young gunman called Allan Rudd were driving down the road in a hot car. They had a 12-shot .22 target pistol. Another car was trying to overtake them, Peter was driving and his mate was in the passenger seat with the pistol. The car tried to pass and Peter yelled: 'Six shots rapid fire,' and the other chap blasted away. The nickname has stuck.

Peter Allen, Dennis and Billy Webb all got pinched in 1973 for robberies, rapes and shootings. In the early days, Peter used to conduct his own legal battles in court to great effect. I must say that without a shadow of a doubt he was Pentridge's foremost jailhouse lawyer.

Before I went down to face the jury at my murder trial, I saw Peter Allen in another cell and he wished me well, and he meant it. He and I were very good friends in the early '70s but a fall-out I had with Dennis destroyed my friendship with Peter. To be honest, although Peter and I became enemies, we never hated each other.

I fell out with Dennis Allen the way I have fallen out with most people ... I belted him.

It happened in B Division in 1975. From that day on Dennis spent thousands upon thousands of dollars in bloodcrazed plots and plans to have me killed. After he got out of jail and proceeded to build a drug and crime empire the plots and plans and money spent on them became larger and larger and more regular. I can now reveal I owe my life to inside information I received.

My secret was that for some ten years I had a spy in the Allen camp. Her name was Tracey Glenda Warren.

Dennis would get into fits of suspicion and paranoia over me and bash, pistol whip and in some case even kill people close to him over his paranoia. For years he searched in vain for the spy. He even thought for a while that I had his house in Richmond bugged, as I was prewarned of every move he made and every death plot he hatched.

But most people have a weak spot. Dennis did the bulk of

his thinking with his dick and Tracey, with her blonde hair and 38-24-34 figure, would 'console' him ... whereupon he would tell her all his troubles. She was never my girlfriend; there was never any sexual relationship between us. She was ten years younger than me and I've known her since she was 14. She was, and still is, a friend.

Why did she do it? Basically, Dennis Allen gave her the shits. Also, I suppose, being Chopper Read's secret spy in such a dangerous world was a bit of a turn-on. Some ladies like the excitement of life-and-death danger. She would ring me in jail, visit me, send me telegrams and come and visit me. God, I knew every move the Allen family made, or were thinking of making.

I became a phantom Dennis could never kill. In jail, where the place was ruled by drugs, here was the biggest drug kingpin in Melbourne unable to get me killed.

Every time Tracey would visit Dennis she would find rolls of cash on the floor. Dennis would be high as a kite on speed and very paranoid and forgetful. He had more money and drugs than he knew what to do with. He would hide or leave rolls of cash around the house, in bags in the fridge, under the carpet, rugs and cushions, in drawers, cupboards, wardrobes, under mattresses, in the back pocket of his old overalls and runners. She wouldn't take too much: two or three grand a visit. I was kept in assorted eats and goodies in jail for ages, all on Dennis's money.

For a wealthy and powerful crime boss, Dennis was a bit of

a dickhead. If I needed dough in jail, I would arrange for blokes to approach Dennis with enough personal facts about me to prove they knew their stuff and with a plan to kill me in jail.

Dennis would be highly excited and eager to listen to plots and plans to poison me with cyanide or arsenic, or to put a time bomb in my television.

I pulled heaps out of Dennis without him ever knowing it. My covert agents would plot and plan with him and then be given several thousand to put the plan into operation. My man would visit me and put a nice little sling in my property and then 'see you later'.

In fact, I made quite a nice little earn over the years by sending so-called hitmen to see my enemies with offers to kill me. The deal was always half the dough up front — and half of that went in my pocket. It was too good to ignore.

Mind you, there were real full-on attempts by Dennis and his crew on my life — but Tracey warned me each time.

I needed her sitting on Dennis's knee with her tongue in his ear, and she did a great job. She is a great girl and a blood loyal friend. She is no longer part of that world or involved with the Allen family, and there is no longer any danger to her in being mentioned. I can't write my story without mentioning the bravest little spy and secret agent I ever had. To Tracey, I say thanks.

In late 1983, I befriended a criminal in Pentridge named

Wayne Stanhope, who was due for release. I thought that every crim in Melbourne knew there was bad blood between me and Dennis Allen, so I didn't even bother telling him about it. When he got out, the poor silly bugger teamed up with Dennis.

I was sent to Geelong Prison and Wayne came down to visit me. He wasn't allowed in but not long after he was dead as a doornail.

I was told what happened was that he went to the Cherry Tree Hotel in Richmond with Dennis and mentioned he had been to see his good mate Chopper. Dennis was all very nice about it, saying: 'Oh, I haven't seen old Chopper for years.'

They then went back to Allen's place, where poor old Wayne was shot dead while changing a record. Dennis, in his drug-crazed, paranoid mind, must have thought that Wayne was either totally stupid – which he was – or was being insulting and sarcastic and trying to have a go at him.

He may even have thought Wayne was a Chopper Read plant. I often feel sorry for poor Wayne. What a silly bugger.

Chapter 16

The Russell Street Bomber

'I don't want anyone to think that my friendship with Slim means that I approve of the death of Angela Taylor.'

On March 27, 1986, a stolen car packed with gelignite exploded outside the Russell Street police station. Constable Angela Taylor died from injuries she received in the blast. Craig Minogue was found guilty of her murder and sentenced to 28 years minimum. Stan Taylor, a career criminal, got life.

I HAVE always found Craig 'Slim' Minogue to be a jolly giant. I know that offering kind words about the Russell Street bomber is about as welcome as the Pope at the Masons' picnic, but he really has a lot going for him. Sometimes people say I have a weight problem, and I take offence to that, so I stand next to Slim, who is easily 24 stone, and I feel like a graduate of the Gloria Marshall Academy.

Slim was the force behind setting up the Pentridge Legal Resources Centre, which has been a great help to prisoners and helps them understand the law. I suppose because he is the Russell Street bomber he will never get the credit he deserves for that.

Slim has always maintained that he was not guilty of the Russell Street bombing. I have told Slim that nothing is more boring than people forever flogging the not guilty line: 'I didn't do it, I'm not guilty, it's all a foul conspiracy against me,' and so forth. But I do believe Slim is not quite as guilty as everyone thinks. He was the only man in the dock who truly made no statements whatsoever to police. Personally I wouldn't buy a used lawnmower from the rest of that crew. With friends like that Slim didn't need enemies.

One of the key people was Paul Kurt Hetzel. Hetzel himself was a one-time member of the Overcoat Gang but in 1977, in H Division, he was beaten within an inch of his life and expelled from the gang. Jimmy Loughnan and I found Hetzel guilty of playing all sides against the middle. We felt he was far too treacherous for even our company. He lied to us nonstop and passed on false information which nearly resulted in Jimmy being murdered. When we went into battle Hetzel told the screws he didn't feel well and went to his cell for a lie down where he stayed for a week. So he was beaten and expelled.

Whether Slim is truly guilty or not, only Slim and God would know, but what I do know is that I wouldn't find Adolf Hitler guilty of farting in a public place on the verbal evidence of Paul Hetzel.

The other star Crown witness was Stan Taylor, an old lag who had done half his life in jail already and didn't want to do any more. He gave up Slim and still got life.

The other witness, Zelinka, is just a long-haired hippy bikie. If the case had rested on his evidence, Slim would be out now. I am not saying Minogue is innocent, but just not as guilty as he has been made out to be.

Six were arrested at the start, five went to trial and two were convicted. He was the only one to stay totally silent throughout. Did he do it? Who knows.

Slim is also the most rock solid crim I've ever met. I mean, he wouldn't shout inside a police station if a shark bit him. If he had opened his mouth like the rest of them then he would have been acquitted like the rest of them. You can't count Stan Taylor — he opened his mouth so wide, he fell in it himself.

But I can tell you one rumour about Slim — and that is he might have been one of the last people to see Laurie Prendergast alive.

The rumour that Prendergast got dropped off somewhere along the Great Ocean Road, is just that, a rumour. No one ever listens to them, do they?

Some people might find my friendship with Slim Minogue to be a bit strange considering that I have no time for the Russell Street bombing.

I know all the bombers, and knew Stan Taylor and Paul Hetzel before Minogue had even met them. Out of the bombers who were pinched Slim was the only one who didn't laugh about the death of the policewoman, Angela

Taylor.

The others would laugh and make crude jests about her but Slim did not partake in them. I found the jokes about her death distasteful. Real men do not laugh about the death of some harmless girl.

Slim would walk away from those 'comedy' sessions when they were in progress, and that is when I first noticed him. After a while he expressed his displeasure at such jokes and they stopped.

I don't want anyone to think that my friendship with Slim means that I approve of the death of Angela Taylor.

Ted Eastwood said he could remember Angela Taylor when she was on duty during one of his court appearances. He said she was a really nice, polite young woman.

I don't agree with the Russell Street bombing, either in principle or as a terror tactic. It was ridiculous. It was without stated goal, purpose or reason. A true act of terror requires a man to stand up and say, 'I did that, I did that for this reason and I have friends who will do it again.'

If it was meant to be an attack on the police to weaken their morale, it failed as it only served to strengthen them. As a tactic, it was a mindless fiasco. A ten-minute warning to clear the street should have been issued. If demands had not been met then a second bomb, again with a ten-minute warning.

But Russell Street, along with Walsh Street, must go down as the two greatest weapons the police have been given in their fight against crime, and the men who did it are blunderers of the highest order.

If an action such as Russell Street was carried out by an IRA unit and the planning officer in charge of the operation forgot to give the 10-minute warning, he would be shot.

If a man kills in self-defence or for revenge, or kills a personal enemy I fully agree, but I will not applaud stupidity.

But there is more to Slim than meets the eye. He is a member of several organisations which are connected to the Middle East. He is a member of one Libyan group with connections in Australia and keeps in touch with the Palestine Liberation Organisation in Canberra.

Some groups try to use prisoners to help them pursue their causes. At one time Slim was running around in prison trying to gain support for an 'interest group' on Middle Eastern matters.

He once asked me if I could get in touch with Dave the Jew. He offered to pay for the Jew's time. I roared laughing. With Slim's activities with the anti-Jewish groups I would have thought that the Jew would not be interested in helping Slim with anything.

Chapter 17

The Klan and Other Crazies

'The neo-Nazi and anti-Jewish ratbag groups are stronger than most people imagine ... they are playing with the feeble minds of the lost and lonely.'

What has never been spoken of before is the multitude of political activists and crazy nitwit groups who see prisons as recruiting grounds for their ideologies.

These groups go out of their way to try and manipulate prisoners to hop on this or that bandwagon.

The lost, lonely and bored in here are all looking for something to belong to, and so they are a natural target for the various weird and wonderful religious, social and political ratbag groups in society.

Most of these groups are pretty harmless – everything from Left-wing Commie, Save the Nation via the Teachings of Stalin groups to the Gay neo-Nazi Action Faction.

The neo-Nazi and anti-Jewish ratbag groups are stronger than most people imagine, and prisons are where they recruit some of their more zealous and dangerous followers.

However, the really dangerous groups to watch are the ones from the Middle East. As I have mentioned they are in touch with the Russell Street bomber, Slim Minogue, and a lot of other prisoners.

Slim has a great interest in these matters and is in touch with several groups in Australia connected with the Palestine Liberation Organisation and the Libyan Cultural Centre.

Why? Let's just say that I don't see Slim as someone who would get involved in these sorts of issues just to hand out pamphlets at the PLO Ladies' Auxiliary night.

Minogue's involvement with these groups has been a bone of contention between him and me for some time. No members of the media know about him being in touch with groups sympathetic to the Palestinian and Libyan causes.

The anti-Jewish, racist, neo-Nazi and National Action type groups are very active in prison. These groups send in booklets and pamphlets to help recruit an inmate. Then that prisoner is encouraged to recruit new members in the prison.

Some of these groups can be very helpful. Some of the weirder religious groups send in female visitors to newly signed-up members, to add further encouragement.

Basically, it is playing with the feeble minds of the lost and lonely.

My own view is that the Middle Eastern political groups are wolves dressed in sheep's clothing. I suspect they have a hidden agenda. Some of the groups that Slim is involved with are world-wide. The Australian-Irish groups are heavily involved in recruiting sympathisers in jail and they could be dangerous too.

The more serious Right-wing neo-Nazi groups don't bother dressing in sheep's clothing. They are hate clubs, pure and simple. You will hear more of them as the racial tension inside jails increases. There will be violence.

Within Pentridge and other jails there are several main groups. There are the blacks and the rice eaters broken up into their various secret crews, and the neo-Nazis. There is no real Ku Klux Klan as such, but there are a fair few, including my good self, who joined and hold registered membership in the international brotherhood of the KKK. You can apply for membership via the Imperial Wizard, in America. To me it is a bit of a joke, but there is real racism in jails and it is only going to get worse.

Some of the neo-Nazis are really serious and they have joined the KKK.

After I have gone I think there will be big trouble and bloodshed over it all. There is a group called the AB, taken from an American idea. It stands for Aryan Breed or Aryan Brotherhood. Personally, I would join the Methodist Ladies College All Girl Marching Band if it's to my advantage. In fact, as I have mentioned elsewhere, I always thought it was wise to extend the hand of friendship to some of the future key players amongst the Vietnamese.

In time, the KKK will take on here. What began as a joke

will catch on in the minds of men with long terms to serve and enemies to fight. If so, then the KKK, Nazis, and the others will team up against any other group seen as a threat.

For all that, the picture of me taken with the KKK hood in H Division was just a joke. A joke in poor taste, but just a joke. This is a man's jail, and naturally enough some jokes are in poor taste. If we had a monkey mask we would have worn that. After all, it gets pretty boring in there for all of us, the screws included.

Because of the publicity, some black prisoners have become terrified of what would happen to them if they went to H Division.

In some minds there is a strong KKK out there, but really it is mostly in their minds. But because people have been protesting about it so much and trying to make it into something, the joke will eventually grow into reality and blood will be spilled.

One of the screws photographed with me was Big Peter Prideaux, a bloke with a real Aussie sense of humour, a hard man but a fair man. When Peter and the boys were in H Division the place ran like clockwork. The KKK was a joke created to ease tension. Peter Prideaux will fight anyone toe to toe, fair and square, and is an honest, straight-down-the-line screw with a realistic attitude and that black sense of humour you need to survive in prison. Sadly, his sort are few and far between these days.

Chapter 18

A Headache for Alex

'He was just a total, ruthless crazy bastard who always wanted to kill.'

Ruthless businessman Alex Tsakmakis entered the world of heavyweight crime when he was convicted of the murder of professional runner Bruce Walker in 1978. He went on to burn fellow Jika Jika inmate Barry Quinn alive in 1984.

According to Read, Tsakmakis boasted of being involved in several unsolved murders. They include the 1978 Manchester Unity St Patrick's Day massacre of jewellers Paul Pace, Robert Waterman and Keith Hyman, and the murder of prostitute Margaret Clayton, found shot twice in the head in a North Fitzroy massage parlour in June 1979. Tsakmakis also claimed credit for the murder of Willie Koeppen, owner of The Cuckoo restaurant in Olinda, who disappeared on February 26, 1976, and whose body has never been found. Tsakmakis told Read he killed National Gallery curator Brian Finemore, whose body was found in his East Melbourne flat on October 24, 1975, 80 minutes before he was to meet Princess Margaret to guide her through the gallery.

Tsakmakis was killed in H Division by the Russell Street

bomber, Craig Minogue, in 1988. Minogue swung a laundry sack
containing two gym weights, each weighing 2.25 kg, and hit
Tsakmakis over the head at least three times.

Tsakmakis didn't stand a chance. His head was pulped, and he
died from massive brain injuries.

I first met Alex Tsakmakis in H Division in 1980, just
before Alex, Ted Eastwood and I went to Jika Jika. I was
the first into the division, Ted was next and Alex third.
We were sent to the maximum security section of Jika. I
remained there for three solid years of total madness. The
time was filled with violence and physical and emotional
torment. Eastwood was sent to another division after a period
of weeks, leaving Alex and me behind.

To cut a long story short, Tsakmakis and I had words,
resulting in me having to teach Alex some manners with a
pair of scissors in the back of the neck. He lived and ran
screaming with blood pissing from the wound. I pleaded
guilty, but I said I was provoked and got a short sentence.

Tsakmakis and I became blood enemies until years later,
when we called a halt to our hatred and joined forces to fight
a common enemy.

We were a powerful team for a while. Tsakmakis was a
millionaire, a wealthy businessman on the outside who was
willing to put his money where his mouth was in relation to
getting the job done. I took care of tactics. However, he was a
power-mad psychopath who gave me word-for-word details

of his part in the Manchester Unity murders and assorted other killings. He had a hit list inside and outside jail and had ordered, paid for and planned crimes of violence on the outside while he was still in jail.

He told me about some of the people he killed, including Margaret Clayton. He claimed she was the only woman he had ever killed. There was the old couple he shot at the Tansiotto agency in Hawthorn, but they lived, so I suppose he was right.

He went into some detail about one bloke he killed who was connected to the market garden industry, some wealthy old bloke well known at the Victoria Markets. Tsakmakis said he had been killed in the dark in the early morning.

Another fellow he killed, a wealthy businessman, won a large amount of cash from Alex in a card game. Alex flattered himself he was a great card player, and so anyone who beat him was a cheat as far as he was concerned.

He also told me he had killed a bloke in the automotive industry. Tsakmakis owned a company which made car ramps and he was ruthless with competition. He was well known when he was out and feared in certain circles in the automotive industry. He had a reputation as a man who would burn out his opposition.

He was just a total, ruthless crazy bastard who always wanted to kill. In jail his main topics of conversation were money, cards and revenge. He was always talking about the murders he hoped to commit.

He used to talk so much about all the violence it went in one ear and out the other. Or so to speak ... I don't have any ears.

Alex had trouble hiding his light under a bushel. He would tell you what he did, but he wasn't stupid. He would always keep back certain details which would prove he did it in a court of law. He was, by nature, a true coward, but also a sadist with a massive ego. I didn't think I would ever meet anyone with an ego as big as mine, but I can laugh at myself, whereas Alex took himself very seriously.

A coward, a sadist and an egotist is a very, very dangerous mixture. He would not act out of courage or bravery, but as a result of feeling threatened or frightened, or as a result of hurt pride or damaged ego.

I remember in Jika Jika, before I stabbed Alex, I had a fight with another prisoner in Unit 2, a chap called Mick Windsor doing life for murder. I beat the bugger half to death, mainly with knee blows to the face and head. There was blood everywhere. I ended up with fluid on the knee as a result of the blows I gave the bloke as he lay helpless on the door.

Alex, who was standing well out of the way, ran forward with a gleam in his eye, bent down and broke the fellow's arm at the elbow. I mean to say, I belted the poor chap, who I didn't have a thing against personally, as a favour to Alex, as Alex didn't have the guts for hand to hand combat. Tsakmakis wanted to kill him because Mick had drunk some water out of his cup. That's how crazy the mad Greek was: he wanted to kill over a cup of water.

While the poor chap lay helpless on the floor with his left arm broken at the elbow, Alex wanted to kill him. This was in full view of some prison officers. I stepped in and lifted the half-conscious fellow up, tossed him against the door and signalled to the prison officer, who was watching the whole thing while eating a piece of fried chicken, to push the remote control button. This was to open the door so that I could push the poor devil out of harm's way.

But Alex wanted more blood. He was by now in a killing frenzy. I thought to myself, 'I'll handle this Greek' and whopped a half a dozen more uppercuts into poor Mick. Then the screws opened the door in a hurry and I was able to push him out, away from Tsakmakis. What the poor bastard wouldn't know is that I probably saved his life, although I doubt that he would thank me.

I was charged and punished over it, and I even took the blame over the broken arm. Alex would have lost visiting rights and I didn't have any at the time, so what the heck. But Alex is dead now, and I don't like the idea of people thinking that I would do anything as cruel and sadistic as that. I don't carry on with violence against a whimpering, fallen victim. To kill an opponent in combat, fair enough, but to torment, torture and kill for no sane reason after your opponent has already fallen, that is not the act of a man.

Just because you are going to kill a man is no excuse for

bad manners. I belted that poor guy because he drank out of Alex's cup, which was a no no. Alex wanted to have his revenge but, to be honest, Mick Windsor would have punched 10 shades of shit out of Alex. Had I not agreed to act, Alex would have killed him from behind – and I didn't need that bullshit over a cup of water, so I ripped into Windsor and gave him a touch-up. But for big, brave Alex to break his arm was a cowardly thing.

Why did I later stab Alex and not just punch his head in? Because when the big pair of scissors came into the yard Alex claimed them as his. So here I had a mass killer, a coward, sadist and egomaniac walking around with a big pair of scissors. One day he had his back to me, standing up reading the *Financial Review* – Alex had it sent in for him, the posh bastard. Anyway, he was leaning over with a hand on either side of the open paper, and the scissors beside his right hand. I walked up behind him saying, 'What have you got there, the funny pages?' I leant over his shoulder, snatched up the scissors and stabbed him in the neck.

I later dipped my fingers in his blood and wrote on his cell door, 'Sorry about that, Alex.'

But Alex did teach me to play chess – and for that I thank him.

I suspect he killed more people than anyone knows. He was killing from about 1973 onwards. He said he was the person behind the murder of that German restaurant owner up in the hills, the bloke whose body has never been found. I

Taking aim at my critics.

One of my mates, mad Charlie, who was murdered.

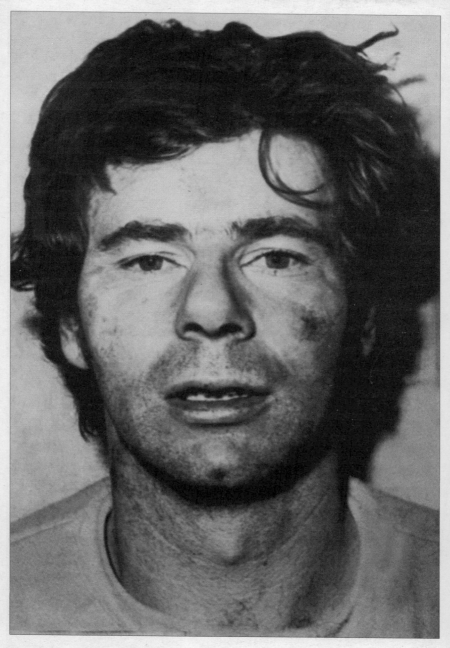

Jimmy Loughnan – he was like a brother to me. I learnt a lesson when he stabbed me with a razor.

Top: A rooftop prison riot.

Below left: Jimmy Loughnan during a prison riot and, *right*, having broken both ankles after trying to escape for the third time.

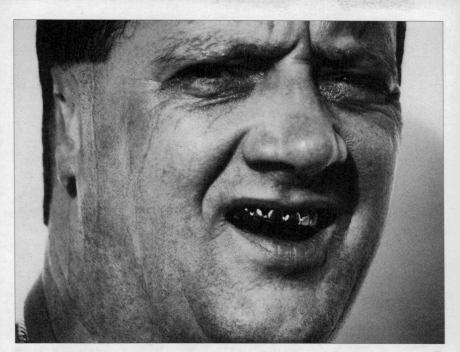

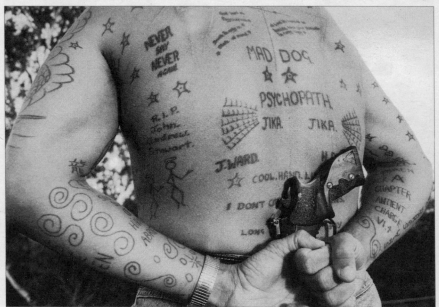

Behind that charming smile…

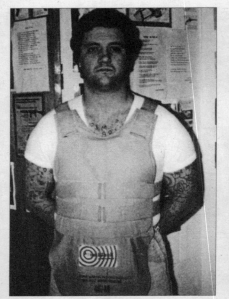

Top left: In the vest I got from the armed robbery squad.

Top right: With my dogs, Ronnie and Reggie, named after the Kray twins.

Below: With Gilbert, a big drug dealer.

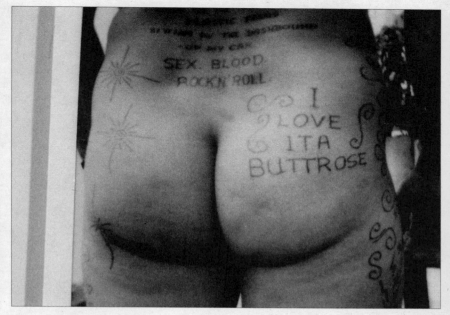

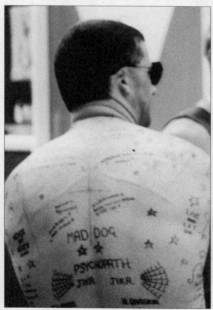

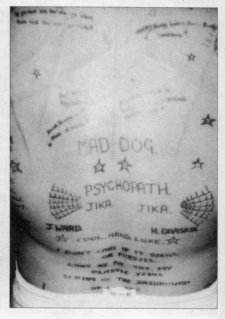

Top: Don't go making me the butt of any of your jokes.

Below: Chopper's back.

Stills from the film *Chopper*. Top Aussie comedian Eric Bana played the part of me.

© *Metrodome*

remember Tsakmakis said the bloke owed him money, and there was a falling-out. I think it was him who got the bag of lime funeral. Alex was into that murder up to his neck. He was proud as a peacock over that one.

He told me he killed a poof well-connected in Melbourne social circles. Some bloke connected in the art world. He was found murdered in a Fiat. The bloke was connected to the art gallery in St Kilda Road. Alex had some stolen art work he was trying to sell, two statuettes and a painting, but this bloke was honest and was going to tell. Alex 100 per cent took credit for that murder.

He was, in my opinion, an ultra-violent character with a Napoleon complex.

He saw himself as a truly great man, and had no sense of humour to go with it. He was an insufferable personality. While we were on the same side, I knew that one day he would turn on me. I knew that my attack on him some years earlier in Jika Jika was not forgotten or forgiven and sooner or later he would seek revenge.

We had done a lot of jail together. I knew him too well and I knew too much about him; sooner or later I would have to go.

When Craig 'Slim' Minogue, the Russell Street bomber, entered H Division Alex and I arrived after the Jika fire. In H Division I again teamed up with Alex. He was called the barbecue king as a result of burning Barry Robert Quinn to death at Jika.

Although I had teamed up with Alex, I had also become friendly with big Craig. It was about this time I learned that Alex had been offered $7000 to stab me. The offer was made by a drug dealer I had fixed on the outside. I waited, thinking that Alex would tell me of the contract. However, Alex was a money-mad bastard who was also power crazy. Revenge over my stabbing him was long overdue, so here we were, supposedly a team, with one planning to kill the other. I had a small problem.

It was at this time that Tsakmakis came to me with a plot to attack and kill Craig Minogue. This was typical: his whole life was made up of violence and plots of violence. He saw Minogue as a future threat to his own power base, so he put Minogue on top of his hit list. I agreed, knowing that my agreement to help kill Minogue would help postpone the plot to kill my good self.

Alex had a very fine leather punch spike, and planned to hit Minogue in the back of the neck, hitting the central nervous system. Death with a single blow. I was to mix with Minogue and his team in their yard and check that they were unarmed, at ease and relaxed. I was to clear out of the yard and tip Alex that it was all clear.

I agreed. But when I got into Craig's yard, I warned him of the attack. Alex had planned the attack for months in advance and intended to claim it was self-defence. Here was Alex, planning with me to kill Craig and at the same time planning with a third party to kill me. He had also accepted another contract to have a B Division prisoner, Trevor Jolly, killed. And I was warning Slim Minogue. It was an ultra-dangerous game of human chess. One wrong move could mean death.

I was the laundry man. I was working in the laundry yard. I mixed with Craig and his crew for a few hours in the morning in the exercise yard.

Craig used to come down to the laundry yard to see me daily, as did Alex. I placed one of my boys, Joe 'The Boss' Ditroia, in Craig's yard to mix with him and his crew. Joe was armed with an ice pick most of the time. He worked with me in the laundry yard as a rule but I had him mix with Craig's crew to guard me against counter-treachery from that quarter. Craig's right-hand man Peter Michael Reed didn't like me. So you have the picture: a total nest of vipers, treachery and counter-treachery.

Alex was the food billet. Craig had a bad habit of allowing Alex to stand behind him after Alex put the food down. It was at lunchtime that Alex planned to make his move on Craig. But on the day, I warned Craig it was coming, then got out of the yard and went back to my cell about 20 minutes before Alex was due to take the lunch tray down. Alex came to my cell and asked me through the trap door if everything was sweet. I said yes, that they didn't have a weapon in the yard and they suspected nothing. I then borrowed two cartons of smokes from Alex and lay on my bed and watched television. Half an hour later I heard all the fuss, then a screw opened my door and smiled and said: 'You shifty bastard, Chopper.'

Maybe it was because I came up from the exercise yard early or maybe he just guessed that I might have known what had just happened. Alex stepped into that yard ready to kill and he made his move on a man who was totally prepared.

Alex was a truly dangerous bastard, but what I still can't understand was his logic – or lack of it. He was a tactical retard. He allowed his wellbeing and personal safety to be placed in my hands; the hands of a man he was plotting to kill.

Poor old Alex plotted and planned to kill every day. He was a total nutcase, and his mistake in placing me in his confidence over his planned attack on Minogue cost him his life. Considering that he planned to kill me, I thought it was the Christian thing to do. Ha ha.

Alex's death was the end of an era in Pentridge. To allow him to have killed Minogue would have meant that I would have been next. He saw himself becoming the undisputed king of Pentridge. He was the financial backing behind drug sales in B, A and D Divisions. He was pulling in about $1,000 a week profit for himself after wages and expenses. He arranged bashings from one end of the jail to the other. He would set them up and collect payment. He saw Minogue and then myself as the last two stepping stones he needed to reach his own insane glory. None of us in H Division saw Alex's death as anything other than an act of God.

God bless the name of Craig Minogue. Killing Tsakmakis should get him to heaven, all sins forgiven.

Tsakmakis had an evil mind. Myself and Slim Minogue were gentlemen of the old school compared with him.

My warning to Minogue forged a bond between us, something I learned to appreciate later when another party approached him in H Division in relation to killing me. Minogue alerted me. Not only that but he's a brilliant jailhouse cook. I put on two and a half stone in H Division over 12 months eating food he cooked.

What a nuthouse.

Chapter 19

Julian Beats the Death Penalty

'Mass murderers come and go ... but good soldiers are hard to find.'

Julian Knight will live in infamy as the man who went mad in Hoddle Street, killing seven people and injuring 19 others in 1987. He was sentenced to 27 years for the slaughter.

Knight, a former officer cadet at Duntroon Military College, had been ordered out of the College after stabbing another cadet at a Canberra nightclub.

On the evening of August 9, 1987, Knight left his adoptive mother's house in Ramsden Street, Clifton Hill, armed with a .22 rifle, an M14 military rifle and a shotgun.

He then walked around the area and in 40 minutes shot at anything that moved, killing and wounding as many people as he could. He also shot at the police helicopter, which was forced down.

Knight, slightly built and reasonably intelligent, has always been fascinated with guns and military tactics.

Despite the fact that he is a mass murderer, he still does not see himself as a criminal.

But there is another side to Knight which has never been

revealed. As a teenager he used to delight in dressing in the 'bovver boy' garb of English National Front hoodlums – a group of violent right-wing fanatics. The question of how such a person was accepted as a candidate to train as an officer in the Royal Australian Army has never been answered.

I don't agree with what Julian Knight did in Hoddle Street and, now, he doesn't agree with what he did, either. I tend to think you either hang him or leave him in peace – but don't torment him in the prison system. Strangely enough, I have found him to be a loyal friend. He certainly isn't a poof, which has been hinted at in some quarters.

That said, let me reveal that it is only by the grace of God – with just a little bit of help from me – that Julian is still alive today. The fact is, he came within a hair's breadth of being executed not long after he got to jail. The kangaroo courts we have in prison aren't as forgiving as the law courts.

It happened like this. When Julian arrived in H Division he made the mistake of trying to impress everybody by flashing his murder photos around – meaning the pictures taken at the scene of the Hoddle Street massacre by police for evidence at court.

I've seen some bad sights, but the photos of these innocent people with their faces blown away were terrible. One poor lady had her whole face, nose, mouth, chin, forehead and eyes simply blown off. The .308 bullet entered at the back of the skull and went through her head.

It was all too much for us. My right-hand man, Joe 'the Boss' Ditroia, wanted to put an ice pick through the back of Julian's skull. In fact, we all considered putting Julian to sleep. The screws even agreed to turn a blind eye if we decided to finish him off.

So, you see, it was touch and go. However, Julian put his photos away and Craig Minogue had a talk to him and tried to put him right on a few points and all was well. Funny thing, when Craig has a talk to people out here they tend to listen.

On the other hand, Joe the Boss was far from convinced that Knight had learned his lesson and was still looking for any excuse to kill him. But Joe had a small problem with carrying out the killing. After he had stabbed Sandy Macrae they had taken all his ice picks and knives from him.

Around that time Joe was quite kill happy. He was always saying: 'Can I kill Knight, Chopper, can I please?' I would say, 'No, he's on our side. He always wanted to be in the army – well, he's in Chopper's army now.'

I told Joe that we could send Julian out in our battles and that if he got killed, then it would be fair enough, but we wouldn't kill members of our own crew. Joe finally agreed after a lot of grumbling. Joe was a bloodthirsty little customer. He had previously stood over Alex Tsakmakis' fallen body, eating a plate of spaghetti, waiting until the screws rushed in. Joe didn't mind a bit of blood, but he did what I told him and that's why Julian is alive now.

But Joe couldn't help thinking about getting Knight. While I was away fighting my murder trial, Joe hatched his own murder plot. He went into the labour yard with Julian. It is fair to say that Julian obviously wasn't too bright to get caught in there.

Joe wanted to start a fight. He suggested it was only because Julian was part of Chopper's crew that he wasn't being regularly raped in the showers. Joe threw in a few more taunts of a sexual nature and Julian flipped out.

Screaming and ranting with rage, Julian picked up a chair and attacked Joe. Joe was shot a few years ago when escaping from Geelong Jail, leaving him with a badly shattered left arm, which still carries a big pin in it. This means that when it comes to a punch on or a knife fight he is a bit of a one-armed bandit. Anyway, with his one good arm, Joe disarmed Julian and then ripped a few right hooks into him. Julian responded by scratching Joe's face like a woman. When the screws came in Julian ran out. Joe yelled after him: 'I'll kill you; I'll kill your whole family.'

Joe was a bit excited by this time. His eye fell on Minogue and he said in a rage: 'You fat slug, you're off as well. I'll fix you all! When Chopper gets back you're a dead man, Minogue.'

Thanks for that little effort, Joe. Fine, great and wonderful. Here I was in court on a murder charge and Joe gets me involved in murder threats. I came back and went into the yard with Slim Minogue and he told me all about it. The screws said Joe was mad.

It was all a mess, but I patched things up by making them all say they were sorry, like naughty schoolkids. I got Julian to apologise for attacking Joe. He apologised to me, not to Joe. Then Joe apologised to me for all the trouble − but he still hated Slim and Julian, calling them the Laurel and Hardy of Pentridge.

Joe wanted to see Julian and Slim dead; he wanted to see everyone dead. He even asked me if I wanted him to stab Russell Cox, after he read somewhere that we were supposed to hate each other.

At the same time Slim wanted to kill Joe. What a mess. But I loved little Joe the Boss. He was as mad as a hatter, but he was loyal to me.

Slim and me had teamed up. I couldn't allow this rather powerful friendship to become upset by some kill−crazy little half-Italian, so I spoke firmly to Joe and demanded that he stop all the kill talk and say sorry to everyone. Joe was due to go back to South Australia in a short while so the crew got back together with a very shaky peace.

Thinking back, it probably wouldn't have hurt to have Joe kill Julian. Ollie the German, who helped make our weapons inside, was first for letting Joe kill Julian. Then he was with me, saying he should live. Ollie would agree to anything as long as it didn't lead to him being stabbed.

It was a nutty crew back then. Later, Julian went to J

Division and I got Ted Eastwood to look after him. The whole idea was to turn a mass murderer into our own personal mass murderer. But Julian was not what I would call a heavy thinker. He had a heap of wonderful points and would be a top addition to any jail gang, but when he went to K Division he was placed in the same unit as the Crown witness in the murder trial that my friend, Frankie Waghorn, was facing. Julian knew this – but the big-deal mass murderer failed to take any action.

I tolerate Julian, but if he had been in the Surrey Road gang, he'd be eating lit cigarettes, drinking vodka and getting a bashing every weekend. Dave the Jew would have put him on the missing list after a month.

In his own way Slim liked Julian too, but he always resented the fact that Julian got less jail than him. Left to their own devices, Slim, Joe and Julian would have killed each other and Ollie the German would have made a huge profit selling ice picks to all sides.

In jail Julian is learning and growing into a sensible young man. He was just a stupid young kid when he was in my crew and, for some reason, Slim and I felt sorry for his situation and we got hold of him before his mind got too perverted by the drug gangsters in here.

Slim is a strong friend, a thinker and a cold-blooded, hard man. Julian might be a mass murderer but he hasn't got a drop of real cold blood in him. On the streets I'd take a dozen Joe the Bosses over a thousand Julian Knights.

Joe had guts, dash and loved blood. He has a big mouth that gave me an earache, but a big heart to go with it. I saw the look of sheer delight when he put that ice pick in Sandy Macrae's back. Joe loves blood and in the end that's the key. Mass murderers come and go but good soldiers like Joe are hard to find.

Because Julian became part of my small crew in H Division it was only normal that when he went up to J Divison he would team up with Ted Eastwood, a long-time and loyal friend of mine. In other words, Eastwood looked after him.

Julian and myself share an interest in firearms and military history and he has a great depth of knowledge on both topics.

Julian has become a penfriend to my father in Tasmania. The mind boggles at the contents of those letters. But, as my father is an ex-army man himself, I think he feels for Julian.

It is hard to defend the indefensible, but Hoddle Street aside, Julian is a nice chap, a solid and loyal friend who knows the rules and doesn't talk out of school and can take what is dished up to him like a man.

Whatever demon or insane monster gripped him on the night he went to Hoddle Street with his guns, it no longer possesses him. I've mixed with killers for 20 years and Julian is no cold-blooded killer, nor is he a head-banging psychopath. He was a kid who flipped out.

He calls me the mentor to the mentally ill. He says it in jest but I don't think he's in any position to be casting doubt on my mental health.

One more thing. Not many people know this, but in 1986 Julian used to get around the city with the Neo-Nazis as an 18-year-old, dressed up like those skinheads in England.

He was recruited by some nitwit Nazi group that was getting around at the time. He told me he was introduced to them by some young bucks he met in what he said was the Prince of Wales Light Horse Regiment in the reserve based in Carlton. He was a member of the army reserve from November 1985 to January 1987. He started off in the training squadron then transferred to B Squadron, employed as a signaller in Squadron HQ, and as an assault trooper in the assault troop.

I couldn't get into the army because I was too 'violent' but they accepted a fascist sympathiser into the Duntroon officers' course. Maybe I wasn't right-wing enough for them. It makes you wonder.

Chapter 20

Mad Dog Cox

'He is the most peaceful so-called killer I've ever met.'

Russell 'Mad Dog' Cox is one of the biggest names in Australian crime. He escaped from Long Bay's maximum security Katingal division in 1977 and spent 11 years on the run with his de facto wife, Helen Deane. Cox, an accomplished armed robber, was serving a life sentence for the attempted murder of a prison officer when he escaped.

A vegetarian and fitness fanatic, Cox was known to run 15 kilometres a day with his dog, Devil.

He was born Melville Schnitzerling on September 15, 1949, and nicknamed 'Tim' by his family because he was the smallest. In 1972 he started using the name Russell Cox. According to police intelligence, he once tapped a telephone line into a police station so that he could be up to date on the search for him.

Cox is a keen student of bushrangers and was an avid reader on Ned Kelly and the 'Wild Colonial Boy' and other bushrangers.

Cox was a master of disguise and kept books with chapters on theatrical makeup. He was caught in Melbourne in 1988 with another NSW prison escapee, Raymond John Denning, who *turned out to be a police informer.*

Cox was sentenced to five years in 1989 on charges of using a firearm to resist arrest and reckless conduct endangering life. He was acquitted of the murder of Painter and Docker, Ian Revell Carroll, who was killed in Mt Martha in 1983.

For quite a few years now there have been rumours and rumblings from Melbourne and Sydney of trouble between myself and Russell 'Mad Dog' Cox, rumours and stories re Cox going to kill me and me out to kill Cox. Police have even jumped on this bandwagon, believing it to be true.

I'm glad to say that Cox and I got to clear the air in H Division in 1991. Both understanding that we have been victims of a scallywag rumour mill. Personally, I have found Coxy to be quite a nice chap, considering he is a vegetarian, a yoga freak, and a bit of a greenie.

I've nicknamed him the 'skinny hippie' and the 'Gloria Marshall Graduate', and he thinks I'm a comical nutcase. Instead of murdering each other we've had quite a giggle over it all. We suspect the rumours were started in the hope that one would kill the other, or we'd kill each other. But that was not to be.

We both feel there are people out there who are broken-hearted that Coxy and myself have gotten together. Russell Cox ended up taking over all the cooking in the laundry yard. It's curried veggies for breakfast – on toast, curried veggies and noodles for lunch and curried vegies and cheese for tea. When I sit on the toilet at night it's like a Bombay hurricane. I'm starting to wonder if the rumours that Coxy wanted to kill me were true after all.

My small stomach ulcer protests violently and I wash it all down with hot coffee or iced water, to try and settle my guts. Coxy's had the laundry yard smelling like Calcutta. I'll walk out of here looking like Mahatma Gandhi. His jailhouse curries with garlic and paprika are so hot, you don't know if you're eating meat, fish or veggies. Craig Minogue, where are you when I need you? Even one of Slim's tuna fondues sounds good.

Cox can't walk past a frypan without wanting to shake hands with it. The first thing I'm having when I get out is a big steak with chips, eggs and mushrooms and some good old Aussie tomato sauce. I will do bodily harm to anyone who comes near me with a curry. The things I've had to suffer in the name of good manners. Jailhouse lawyers and cooks, they will be the death of me.

I don't know if there is such a thing as a cooking psychopath, but I'm starting to wonder about Coxy. The man is possessed. But the curry lunches do have their moments. The other day Russell invited a mate of his, Peter Clune, to lunch at the laundry yard. Clune had just been convicted over armed robberies. We sat there eating one of Russell's curries, the sweat pouring out of us.

Peter was telling Russell about how much money he made

from the armed robberies. He said that at one time he was driving a Porsche that he paid $93,000 for in cash.

Without missing a mouthful of curry I mumbled, 'I wish I had known you then,' and gave a little giggle. Both Russell and Peter looked at each other, then at me. 'What did you mean by that, Chopper?' asked Russell. Realising that I had said the wrong thing I said, 'Oh, I've never ridden in a Porsche before.'

As the conversation continued on money, I looked down at Peter's feet and asked, 'What size shoes do you take?'

That was it. Peter said, 'A man gets convicted of bank jobs one day, gets invited to lunch the next, only to have his stomach set on fire with an Indian curry while Chopper Read cracks toecutter jokes. I'm not coming to the restaurant again.'

The toecutter is the natural enemy of the bank robber. That is why the friendship between Russell and I is a strange one. But Peter Clune is a friend of a mate of mine in Tassie, so his feet are safe under the old mate's act. Clune's mob made a million or two but where has it got him? He says he is broke, but I'm not so sure. He sits in here with a half-finished hair transplant. Most of those in the criminal world end up broke, dead or dying day by day.

Even Coxy agrees that if you walk across a busy street back and forth, you'll get bowled over in the end. Clune's nickname inside is 'Piggy Bank Pete' as we suspect he really does have plenty of dollars. I joke to the boys that Piggy Bank

Pete should be put under heavy questioning. He laughs and says that he is just an honest tax avoider.

Although I have put a lot of shit on Sydney crooks the exception is Russell. Coxy is probably the greatest bank robber in the history of the nation. America had Willie Sutton and we have Russell Cox. Coxy puts his hero, Ned Kelly, to shame. But in the real world of blood and guts violence, Russell would front up with a note from his mother saying he could not attend. He is a top bloke and the only Sydney crook that I like. But 'Mad Dog' is a nickname the police or reporters gave him down here and, I can tell you, he was badly named.

Russell is a warm-hearted, wouldn't-hurt-a-fly type. He is polite, good mannered and gentle natured. He admits he did all his fighting from a distance of about six feet with a gun in his hand. Blood and guts, rip-tear violence was not his cup of tea whatsoever. For a man with such a violent reputation I have found him to be a friendly, non-violent fellow.

He loathes the mainstream prison population as much as I do. For two men who lived with stories and rumours that one was going to kill the other, it is quite funny the way things have worked out. We both hate the two-bob-type gangsters in the criminal world and we both hate drugs and the men who deal in them.

We are both well read – him more than me – and we have some 'interesting' conversations. He knew Jimmy 'The Pom' Driscoll years ago and he was a great friend of Ray Chuck.

Intelligent conversations are hard to find in prison so I like talking to Russell. I am glad we got together and sorted out fact from fiction.

It would have been sad to have to kill a good bloke because of some bullshit rumour. He was told that I was out to kill him and I was told that he was going to kill me. We both felt that our first meeting would be in the streets with guns blazing. I didn't know it at the time, but in 1987 some crims were taking bets and giving odds on who would kill who first. The whole thing got right out of hand. Now that we are friends, the only thing that Coxy and I fight about is when he puts too much garlic in our lunchtime curry.

Russell's favourite song is the 1964 classic, 'King of the Road' by Roger Miller. He sings it over and over to himself when he is cooking. I suppose for the 11 years he was on the run he really was the king of the road.

Russell used the name Mr Walker when he was on the run. He liked the name because it was the code name used by the Phantom in the comic book series. Russell's dog, Devil, even had a code name. He was known as Butch when they were on the run.

Russell was always cool. He was pulled over for licence checks and breath tests and was never fazed. Once, when there were police screaming all over the place, he just drove on. The police didn't notice the dog running after the car. Russell just opened the door of the car and Devil jumped in, barking out the back window at the police, who were blissfully unaware.

On the day Russell was caught it was one of the few times he didn't heed the advice of his beloved wife, Helen. She said, 'Don't go, I have a bad feeling about it.' Raymond Denning was there. Denning is a dog but Russell doesn't blame anyone but himself. Regardless of how treacherous Denning turned out to be, the fact was Russell failed to take notice of the alarm bells he heard in his head and the warning he got from his wife. Denning was a police informer – a dog. But a dog can't bite you unless you drop your guard.

There is something almost Zen in Russell's thinking. What will be, will be. It is all in the hands of fate. He is the most peaceful so-called killer I have ever met, and one of the most interesting people I have known.

Not many people know that the turning point in Russell's life came when he was just ten years old. He had the winning ticket in a raffle for a brand new, beautiful bike. He wasn't at the draw, but he was told by some other kid that his number had won. Filled with boyish excitement he ran to town to collect his prize. When he arrived he held his ticket in his hand and said that he had won. 'Here's my ticket – where's my bike?'

The man in charge told him he was too late and because he wasn't at the draw, the bike had been raffled again. The kid protested in vain, but was sent away empty-handed. So he stole a brand new bike and told everyone he had won it in a raffle. However, he never forgot being cheated out of the bike.

The turning point in my life was never so clear, but I think Russell's story would bring a tear to a glass eye.

Personally I think he has had better luck on his worst days than I've had on my best. He even won $15,000 on Tattslotto when he was on the run, and collected it. Jesus Christ, I've shot people for less money than that.

RUSSELL

There was a wild Australian boy,
Russell was his name,
He was born in Sydney town,
Five miles from Balmain,
Born to be an outlaw,
He loved robbing banks,
He loved to rob the money,
And tell the tellers, 'Thanks,'
The coppers missed him a hundred times,
He left them in a mess,
With Russell running down the street,
Wearing a lady's dress.

Chapter 21

Russian Roulette with Rice Eaters

'I have every reason to believe the balance of criminal power in Australia will tilt towards Asian gangs in the next ten years.'

I've made money with a gun in my hand a lot of different ways. But the strangest of all was when I was invited to a Vietnamese pool hall in Footscray to play that stupid 'Deer Hunter' game.

The Vietnamese love to play games and gamble, and they love blood – especially somebody else's. So no wonder they like this game: they can bet on whether someone is going to blow his brains out or not, right there in front of them.

Some white fellas were challenged to play by the Asians. The whites didn't have the guts to do it, as you have to be totally mad or have a death wish, but I had a go.

The thing is, you can bring your own handgun if you want – and I brought my Ruger Black Hawk single action .44 magnum.

The rules are straightforward. You might even say, fiendishly simple.

The gun is test fired into a stack of phone books, then a fresh bullet is put on the table.

The player picks up the weapon for all to see, pops the cylinder out, puts the bullet in and spins it, puts it to his head, pulls the hammer back ... and pulls the trigger.

I'd do it. Click. Nothing. I would then remove the slug from the gun and hand them both to the rice eater I was playing.

However, I made sure I had a little advantage nobody else knew about. I knew my gun was perfectly balanced, so that if I put a slug in at the top and spun it the right way and snapped the cylinder back, it would snap back with the slug at the bottom. Well, 19 times out of 20, anyway, which is good enough odds for me.

I practised with my gun so that I had the odds on my side. Hours I spent spinning the cylinder, until I worked out that I had the safety edge of about 20 to one. I had faith in my gun, and believed the odds were on my side.

My opponent, who didn't have that edge, was working at six to one.

I may be mad, but I'm not a total fool.

After each spin the bets on the table would go up. The other fellow goes through the same process before firing. What he didn't know was where to place the slug or how to spin the cylinder for safety, so he was playing the game for real, unlike my good self.

I played the game several times and no one died and no

one ever went more than three spins against me. The other fellow would always bail out. The winner would walk away with a good earn for his efforts.

I used to put on a real show. I would always take off my shirt and, as I'm covered in tattoos and scars, they would love it. They would see this bloke with tattoos, razor slash marks all over his chest, back and shoulders, short hair and no ears, and think it was marvellous. They would chatter like excited monkeys. And I would always carry a second gun, a fully loaded .38 automatic in the front of my pants, down my belt. They loved it.

Then, when I put the gun to my head I would take out my teeth and give my Asian opponent a big, crazy smile and pull the trigger.

This is very off-putting. No one wants to play Russian Roulette with a madman.

There is no greater excitement and gut-wrenching thrill than to put the gun to your head, pull the trigger and live through it, to have cheated death.

I would sometimes play on my own and I would always play one round by myself before I went to the game. It made me feel immortal. I know it was unhealthy, but it gave me a thrill to tease death.

What some of the little monkeys didn't realise was that if things had gone wrong for my opponent a lot of the onlookers would have gone too.

Most of the Asian players kept the gun horizontal when

they stuck my magnum against their heads. All the other Viets would crowd around him, ten or 11 deep.

If the gun had gone off the bullet would have passed through my opponent's head and six or seven other skulls before it slowed down. The Viets didn't really understand the power of a .44 magnum. I was about a foot taller, if I had blown my head off the bullet would not have hit anyone else.

To do well in the game you had to be willing to die; you had to 'will' yourself into a state of mind where you were prepared to die. If you play just to make money or to prove how much guts you have, you will lose in the end. You have to be mentally prepared for death before you even walk into the game.

Guts has nothing to do with it; you would will yourself almost into a suicidal state.

The Asians are cool players because they have a different view of death, but in the end they are working on guts, a sense of luck and personal honour. That's why none of them would go more than three turns against me.

The bets were increased after each round. I was promised some money for playing the game. I would win $4,000 to $6,000 when I went there. Once I made $8,000.

It was easy money, in one way. But a handful of games was enough for me. I just didn't trust the shifty bastards.

It is hard to try and explain in a sane manner what is an insane game. Most of the rice eaters went to the game to bet, but the real reason they wanted to be there was to see one of the players blow his brains out.

I often wonder what they would have done if someone had blown their head off ... bury the body, or eat it.

The Asians' fascination with Russian Roulette shows how bloodthirsty they are. Which is one reason why I have every reason to believe the balance of criminal power in Australia will tilt towards Asian gangs in the next ten years. These little fellows have already built themselves a sort of rice-eater intelligence network from Richmond, Springvale and Footscray, right through to Cabramatta in NSW and Fortitude Valley in Queensland.

The head boys of those crews all know each other at an interstate level. They have the contacts. They may be modest now but they will grow in time. Back in Vietnam they all stuck together and they are doing the same thing here. They have different dialects and they even have a Vietnamese slang to throw off any outsiders. Some of the top crews have a sort of Masonic-style symbolism, with ceremonies, code words and secret handshakes.

They all take themselves very seriously. Some of the more powerful teams outside jail have agreed to join forces against common enemies or outside threats. Outside crews look after their members inside, who in turn create a sub-branch in jail. Their ability to find smack is frightening. And as we all know, with that comes power. They also have the brains to know who to approach — namely, my good self, which shows they have scant regard for popularity.

They are concerned only with building a power base. I would say that we will see three of these teams grow to some stature within the criminal world in the areas of drugs, prostitution and gambling.

The Asians' taste for blood is a tad greater than those who control the areas at the moment ... killing the family of an enemy is part of the Asian criminal culture. That's one reason why I would say the little chaps will climb right to the top of the criminal ladder.

At the moment we are seeing violence among their own ranks, and from this several groups will emerge. Then they will reach agreement and from there they will build. At the moment they are looked down upon and laughed at with their childish English and so forth, but that will change. The mainstream criminal world inside and outside jail see them as no possible threat at all. However, I am the exception, hence my extending the hand of friendship to them this early.

The Italians changed the face of the criminal world in Australia in the 1960s with the mafia and the 'black hand' murders in the Melbourne markets. I'll give the rice eaters a few years. By then, mainstream criminals, including the Italians, who have not come to some form of friendly agreement or understanding with these evil little men will have to make their own arrangements, with one eye in the back of their heads.

The Asians are also classic standover merchants. I've stood over clubs, even legal nightclubs in King Street. It is an art form which is not easily learned, but these buggers are masters at it. It is the backbone to their thinking.

Watch them with an eagle eye, and see if I'm wrong. Everyone in the criminal world knows that if they want drugs and they don't want to risk their necks importing their own smack then they have to deal with certain Chinese groups in Melbourne and NSW.

The Vietnamese are not fools and they know more about smack than even the Chinese do. I doubt whether they will ever control everything, but as we are going down the same road as America it's worth noting that the Vietnamese in America have gained wealth and power with frightening speed. I suspect it will happen here with the same speed.

Although I am leaving the criminal world I have made some friends within the Asian criminal scene. I see no harm in this. He might need my help today, I might need his help tomorrow, and in this world survival is the only rule. The one who wins the game is the one who lives the longest. It is a madhouse in prison – and twice as bad outside.

But some of these rice eaters won't have it all their own way. We have all heard that the 'Jap mafia', the Yakuza, is moving into Australia. Well, let me tell you that there are about 14 headhunters scattered around Australia who will have a big say in it.

These men are the real blood merchants of the underworld. I will not name them and they know that. I will tell you that their latest topic of conversation is about these rice-eating chaps. The headhunters are getting bored with continually squeezing the wogs for their money and are looking for a new challenge. They all want that storybook blood war and that is with the Japs.

The Jap crims are the subject of some interesting chat. One fellow I know, a top crim, has told me personally that the first Jap he sees with tattoos or a missing finger, he will cut his head off and put it in a pickle jar.

I mean, it is bad enough the way it is without a bunch of Jap mafia rice eaters swaggering around our beaches and golf courses, flashing their tattoos and picking their noses with their missing fingers. Those blokes will be perverting the morals of nice Aussie girls with their money. Laugh at me, scoff if you like, I know it sounds insane, but mark my words: if the Jap mafia pop their heads up, if they can be pointed out they will go on the missing list, just for the sheer fun of it.

Where is the logic, you ask? That is why the headhunters and blood merchants can't be beaten. There is no logic. You ask why. I say, 'Why not?' The headhunters and blood merchants, though few in number, could be seen as a criminal version of pest control. Criminally speaking we'll put up with the wogs, and tolerate the Vietnamese – but we are not going to cop the bloody Japs, let me tell you.

Chapter 22

Tricks of the Trade

'*A solicitor I'll call The Spider is the keeper of secrets, banker, tax adviser and brains behind the top crime lords. In fact, if he did a runner to South America, most of the drug bosses in town would be on the dole.*'

Here is a secret tactic often used in the criminal world which says it all about the betrayal and hypocrisy which is part of the underworld. It is called the Lemon Twist, and nobody in the straight world knows how it works. A drug gang wishes to maintain its standing in the eyes of the criminal world, yet remain out of jail. They pick a known police informer, some physically weak wimp who is easily frightened. They call him in and explain to him that he now works for them – after a nice little beating, of course.

They then find out from him which police he is working for. They provide him with a weekly sling of money and supply him with a regular line of drugs. He is happy under the protection of the gang. He is given good information on the drug dealings of other gangs and crews. Every bit of information the informer gives to the police is handed to him by his controlling crew. All the information is geared to help the police catch members of other gangs and upset their drug and gambling businesses.

The Carlton Crew have at least four Lemon Twists working for them. It is a closely-guarded but widely-practised trick used by major crews in Melbourne and Sydney. The gangs can control the flow of information and can kill the 'Lemon', or informer, at will. The Carlton Crew have been doing it for about ten years and that is why they have kept out of jail. Some of the old dockies were doing it back in the 1960s. They controlled their own informers and the flow of information.

There are some drug and gambling crews who will never come to jail because of the Lemon Twist. The information given to the police from the Lemon Twist is top notch, so they have to act on it.

There will be a lot of top-notch crews who will be furious that I have tipped a bucket on this old but secret trick, but it is so simple that even a group of drug-crazed retards can put a Lemon together.

It has been used to get some members of the criminal world legitimately shot – killed by the police – without the police ever knowing that their informer was a controlled man and the information he passed on was part of a set-up. The police act on the information in good faith in a 100 per cent legal raid that, in some cases, ends in tragedy. It is simple, smart and deadly.

Lemons are usually drug-dependent and easy to control. They generally get overdosed when they are of no further use. Left alive, they can give the whole game away.

I can talk about underworld tactics because I am walking away from it all. The wise old men of the criminal world know these tricks and the young punks coming up are too stupid to put them together.

One of the most sophisticated tactics is the Apple Cucumber, a little-known and rarely-mentioned trick that I have personally used to great effect.

I first heard of it from the really old crims I met in Collingwood in the early 70s who had been around in Squizzy Taylor's day. Old Horatio Morris spoke of it, and so did The Texan. Now I will explain it.

The Apple Cucumber is to kill or capture your target by using a close friend or family member. I will give you an example. I wish to kill Mr X but Mr X is aware of the plot and is on guard. I steer an agent of mine into Mr X's friend, in a pub, club or race track. My agent is always careful never to mention my name. Mr X's friend and my man become great mates, drinking together, going to parties. My agent may even get to meet Mr X and they may all go out together. Eventually the friend will say to my agent, 'Can I bring my mate with me?' Bingo. I have Mr X where I want him.

The agent tells me that Mr X will be at such and such a hotel at 6.30 that night. My agent meets them for a drink. He walks out one door, I walk in the other ... and that's the Apple Cucumber. Mr X is totally unaware that his life is at risk until it's too late.

The Apple Cucumber is very difficult to detect or escape from. The target is manipulated into a set-up and led to his death by an unsuspecting friend or relative. Brilliant, yet simple. Dead simple.

Behind every smart gangster there is an even smarter lawyer. In Melbourne there is one lawyer who stands at the head of the pile. Let's just call him The Spider.

The Spider was the man who introduced the Melbourne underworld to the three magic words 'Off Shore Banking'. He has set up accounts in Fiji and New Caledonia for assorted crime bosses and underworld personalities. The Spider acts on behalf of Melbourne's criminal establishment, the cream of the crop. The Spider runs the biggest money laundry in Melbourne and in many ways could be called the Meyer Lansky of the Melbourne criminal world. In the mid 1980s he was the first one to start setting up accounts in Tel Aviv.

In fact, if The Spider died, a lot of top drug men and gambling figures would have great trouble finding out where their money was. The Spider acts as a middle man, peace-maker and go-between in the underworld. He is the keeper of secrets, banker, accountant, tax adviser, financial consultant and legal adviser to the top crime lords in Melbourne – the Carlton Crew, Freddy the Wog, The Tiger, just to name a few. If you make big money in the crime world of Melbourne then you talk to The Spider. He hides it for you, washes it for you, cleans it, invests it. He can be seen at certain upmarket auction houses buying for his clients. His office is a neutral ground, often warring criminal factions will meet there to settle a problem with The Spider acting as a middle man. Criminal meetings, even large-scale drug deals, can be set up with him over dinner in some restaurant. He has been under federal investigation and a number of other authorities have had a good look at him, but he is still going strong.

This man is not just employed by drug criminals. He is a part of the top-level criminal scene. In some cases some large-scale money operations have had to be put off because the solicitor was out of the state or country on holidays or on business. I could not overstate this man's power in the criminal world. He knows where the money is and whose it is, and he is the only one who can get to it.

I had a meeting with him once. He wanted to organise a peace meeting between my good self and a crew of crims. I declined. But it shows that if you want someone bribed, or at least an offer made, The Spider is the one to organise it. He is a fixer, a criminal money man. He is the banker and 'Godfather' to many of Melbourne's top drug and gambling men.

He also enjoys the company of young prostitutes and has them supplied to him free of charge. One 15-year-old prostitute was told to tell him she was only 13 to excite him further. He enjoys fine wine, good cigars and top-quality cocaine. He handles a lot of the money from the massage parlour and escort service scene.

When one young criminal felt that some money he had given to the solicitor to wash seemed to have shrunk at the laundry he decided to get even. But the solicitor had the power and the friends, so the young crim ended up being punished. I was asked to do the punishing and, as a favour to a friend, when this young man arrived in jail I dealt with him. On my release The Spider thanked me. Big deal.

What this solicitor just doesn't fully understand is that if I, or any other headhunter, went into real war with any of his clients then he would be the first cab off the rank. He would go into the boot first because, after all, he is the keeper of the financial keys, the brain behind many of the mental retards in the drug and gambling worlds. If he did a runner and fled to South America most of the drug bosses in Melbourne would have to go on the dole.

I have always kept a close eye on him and in 1987, if real war had broken out between some crime crews and me, I fully intended to kidnap or kill The Spider so that the big cash reserves of my enemies would have been frozen, because his secrets would have died with him.

He has become so powerful that he can hardly be stopped. Even if he was struck off and couldn't practise as a solicitor, he would be a full-time financial and tax adviser. His legal law practice has become a yoke around his neck.

I have only ever been caught in a police raid once, and that was in 1974. After that I started to make detailed study of police equipment, police radio codes, and their tactics and strategies. The Special Operations Group is the master of the early morning wake-up call, they have their own codes and signals and are heavily armed. My findings were as follows: spread as much confusing misinformation as acceptable and if that doesn't work, put your hands in the air and smile, for there is no counter move to a surprise.

Hey, no ears doesn't mean no brains.

Chapter 23

Who's Who in the Zoo

John Dixon-Jenkins

One of the most bizarre men ever to enter the criminal world would have to be the self-proclaimed anti-nuclear warrior, John Dixon-Jenkins. He is a campaigner for peace who uses terror tactics to make his point.

In 1991 Dixon-Jenkins was sentenced to 12 years jail over kidnapping seven people in Bendigo jail in 1987.

The quietly spoken, academic-looking man has made it his life's work to try and warn the world of the dangers of nuclear weapons. He was given permission to go on a world lecture tour after he was charged with the kidnapping counts, but jumped bail, forcing police to mount an expensive extradition campaign after he was found in the US.

The man who reputedly had served in the US Navy's atomic submarine service, was sentenced to six years jail in 1984 over a series of bomb hoaxes he made to highlight the anti-nuclear cause.

In 1977 he was interviewed by the US secret service as a potential threat to the then US President, Gerald Ford.

I forget when I met John. I think it was in H Division in 1985. A governor asked me to do him some harm, but I said no. I met John again in Bendigo jail in 1986. I remember I used to tease him a bit and we got on well. He had heard that I could make up poems on request on any topic and I did a poem for him which got published.

I used to do a lot of love poems for prisoners who couldn't do them. They would sign their own names and send them to their girlfriends, wives and mothers. I felt at times like the 'Cyrano De Bergerac' of the prison system.

John Dixon-Jenkins had been in the American navy during the early and middle 1960s and had been sent in along with the American naval SEALS into Vietnam to blow up, kill and create havoc. John called it killing 'friendlies'. It would then be blamed on the North Vietnamese Army. This didn't sit well with John. He felt it was wrong.

He doesn't mention Vietnam much, as he doesn't want to be seen as just another whacked-out headcase left over from the Vietnam war. I can see his point, but by not letting people know, I think he does himself a disservice, as knowing that tidbit can give people a better insight to a complex and, in many ways, brilliant man.

He is, at heart, I believe, a very good man with a gentle nature and a deep concern for the future of the planet and mankind. But I know him personally. I have also seen him snap, which is when you realise he is a man not to be trifled with.

It happened one time at Bendigo Prison. I had to physically hold him back from killing another prisoner because this prisoner had eaten John's ration of icecream. I had to bash the prisoner concerned before John agreed not to commit murder. What people forget is that before he became a peacenik he had killed in Vietnam.

As much as I personally like John, I certainly wouldn't upset him if he was carrying a loaded gun. He is a skilled professional and if you or a thousand others stood between John and his target he would walk over your graves. No, I wouldn't like to see John with a gun in his hand ... nor would I tamper with his icecream ration.

John will no doubt see this as criticsm. All I am saying is that he is not a pretender. He is 100 per cent full-on.

It is not wise to torment or tease a serious man, and John is a very serious man, indeed.

It is a good thing he did not decide to take up a life as a professional criminal — a good thing for everyone.

I first thought of him as a harmless whacked-out Vietnam vet, a peace hippy for the 60s with a difference, 'make peace or I'll shoot you' mentality. But he's quite a strange and unique fellow.

SANITY IN CELL 37

In a world feeding on war and fear,
A world starving of love,

I watched a man drowning in blood and the tears,
Of a sick and dying dove,
A total enigma, a puzzle misunderstood,
Seen as evil in his attempts to do good,
They paid him in torment and emotional pain,
For trying to save us from nuclear rain,
And why, I asked, does he even care,
For a world that cares nothing for him,
Apathy, he answered, that's our greatest sin,
He spoke of a nuclear nightmare that will come upon us all,
It's just a question of time before our Rome will fall,
I read a bit about him and what he was meant to be,
Some said he was CIA, some said he was KGB,
The answer's there, the answer's clear,
But still they fail to see,
He screams words of sanity to the deaf, dumb and blind,
So they locked him away with the criminally ill,
But he's not one of our kind, nor is he a dill,
I see a rage within him others fail to see,
In his utter frustration and the knowledge he can't prevent what
he knows will be,
The anti-nuclear warrior, or the monster from Death Heaven,
The nightmare prophet in cell 37.

Edwin Eastwood

No book on Australian crime would be complete without mentioning Edwin John Eastwood, who was jailed for 15 years for kidnapping teacher Miss Mary Gibbs and six schoolchildren from the Faraday Primary School near Bendigo in 1972.

Eastwood escaped from Geelong jail and kidnapped nine children and seven adults from Wooreen Primary School in South Gippsland, in 1977. He demanded a $7 million ransom before he was recaptured after a high speed chase with police. He was sentenced to 21 years for the second kidnapping.

In 1981 he was charged with killing standover man Glen Joseph Davies in Jika Jika. He was acquitted.

He was released on parole in 1990 but was convicted of factory burglary.

He was sentenced to 12 months jail and his parole was revoked.

In 1979 he completed a religious course run by the Seventh Day Adventist Church and in 1982 he did a Bible study course. In 1985 he was baptised in the jail.

Edwin John Eastwood was the most annoying bastard I'd ever met. When he left Unit Two, Jika Jika to go to another unit and I stabbed Tsakmakis, for some reason, they brought Eastwood back. The trouble was some complete mental case had encouraged Ted towards music.

He came back smiling broadly with his new guitar. So it was that I had to suffer the untold torment of having to listen to hours of him strumming away. Ted always believed he had talent in the music area. What we had was a tone deaf kidnapper, with visions of taking to the stage one day. The first stage out of town, I was hoping.

After some months of this never-ending nonsense, I was at the point of cold-blooded murder. But Ted was a nice guy, despite his lack of musical talent, so I explained to him that if he and his guitar were not out of the unit by the following day I would kill him or kill myself.

Ted was deeply hurt that I felt that he had no musical ability so he and his bloody banjo left the unit.

Later Ted killed Glen Davies in Jika Jika. I was surprised to learn that Davies was strangled to death. I thought when I first heard of his death that he may have committed suicide as a result of Ted's efforts on the guitar.

But as it turned out in court, it was a clear-cut case of self-defence.

Ted came back to Unit Two with me. I looked for the dreaded guitar as he came in but, thankfully, he had sent it out.

Ted and I ended up the greatest of friends in spite of my sarcastic attacks on his musical ability. He is a true gentleman and a loyal friend, a strong man and a rare individual within the prison system and criminal world.

He gave his heart to God and I suspect we will not hear of him again after his release. He has become a Seventh Day Adventist and I can only wish him all the best in the future ... as long as he keeps away from musical instruments.

Vincent Villeroy

Vincent Villeroy died in 1990 in the place of his birth – Londonderry, Northern Ireland. I first met him when he popped in to speak to Ambrose Palmer, the boxing trainer, when I trained at Ambrose's gym when I was 15 or 16. I used to go down to training fairly regularly at the time. I met Villeroy again in the company of an old fighter called Frankie Flannery in 1972, and we had a few drinks with Horatio Morris at the Caulfield Cup in 1972.

Villeroy was a big Irishman with snow-white hair, cauliflower ears and a badly broken nose. He was ex-British Army, boxed as a heavyweight in America, then went back to Northern Ireland and joined the Ulster Defence Regiment. Then he joined the Merchant Navy.

He had fought in the 1939–45 war, had been a prisoner of the Germans, could tell 1,000 stories, and was a jolly, fun-loving, whisky-drinking giant. He reminded me of John Wayne with white hair. He was as rough as guts, but a bloody gentleman. He jumped ship in western Australia, worked in the gold mines at Kalgoorlie, cut cane in Queensland, then settled in Melbourne. I bumped into him again in 1977 after I got out of jail.

He was a great old fellow, as powerful as a draught horse. He would work now and again as a debt collector for some SP bookmakers, and would give me good inside tips about which SP bookies to visit, how much they were holding and where they had it hidden. There would always be a nice drink in it for Vincent.

I met him again in 1987. He was in his early 60s, but still a giant of a man. I had a two-shot .22 calibre Derringer – a tiny little chromed gun that looked like a toy. Vincent was sitting in the front seat of my car and was looking for a light. He looked in the glove box and found my Derringer. He thought it was a nice little lighter. Next thing I knew he had shot himself through the jaw trying to light his cigar.

God, what a bloody mess. But Vincent didn't bat an eye. He said, 'Oh, Chop Chop,' which is what he called me, 'I think I've done myself a mischief.' He was bleeding like a stuck pig from the .22 slug in his jaw. I started to drive him to hospital, but he said: 'Oh, no. Don't bodder wid dat, Chop Chop. We'll clean it up with a dash o' whiskey and you can dig it out for me.'

He was a tough old goat. I got him his Irish whiskey – and some peroxide and penicillin powder. I also got a sharp knife and 'Dr Chopper' did the operation. God, it was a mess. But old Vincent didn't mutter a word of complaint or even flinch.

I got the slug out with chips of bone, washed the wound and cleaned it, then dusted it with penicillin powder. Then I rang a doctor in Collingwood and said my uncle had smashed himself in the face while working on a car – no bullet, no police. There were powder burns, of course, but we would just have to ignore them. And this doctor wasn't too fussy. Anyway, all was well. No fuss, no bother, and no police.

I let Vincent keep the two-shot Derringer as a keepsake. He returned to Ireland in 1988. I heard from him via a postcard wishing me well after I beat the murder blue in 1989, then his brother wrote to me last year telling me he had passed away.

Vincent was a grand old hard man. Top of da morning to him. He's with the angels now.

Dr Bertram Wainer

Dr Bertram Wainer will always be remembered as the man who exposed corruption in the Victoria Police Force in the 1970s. He was born in Scotland, migrated to Australia in 1949, joined the army and then resigned his commission as a Colonel in 1965.

He was the doctor who gathered information that a cell of Victorian detectives were being paid off by abortionists. This resulted in a 1970 Board of Inquiry and Chief Inspector Jack Ford, Superintendent Jack Mathews and Constable Marty Jacobson being jailed over corruption charges.

In 1974 further allegations made by Doctor Wainer resulted in the Beach Inquiry into police.

Wainer died in 1987. Respected journalist and author Evan Whitton described him as a 'man of profound intellect, courage and resource'.

I knew Dr Bertram Wainer throughout the 1970s. He was always good to pull out a bullet or patch up a wound, with no report ever being made to the police.

He was a real anti-police sort of chap and over the years he pulled a few bullets out of friends of mine, patched up shiv wounds, and perhaps wrote out the odd death certificate. Ha ha.

Wainer was bent like a dog's hind leg and charged like a wounded bull. He would only do his medical favours for a certain few. I only got on his list via Horatio. Wainer was a two-faced old goat. Though there was no way he would ever call the police, he was too close to some of Longley's enemies for my liking. If I ever rang him and asked him to bring his little black bag I would always watch for a set-up. I didn't quite trust him. He was a doctor who would pervert himself and his profession for money and a sort of criminal groupie. How could you trust such a man? But he was useful during the 1970s.

Dr Wainer was not a big part of my life, but if mates needed help or I needed it, he was the bloke I'd get out of bed. To be honest, he didn't like me, but he wasn't suicidal either.

Horatio Morris

Horatio Raymond Morris was a big name in the old-style underworld when guts and a gun were more important than drugs and money. He first was convicted on a criminal charge in 1932 and went on to be a professional criminal. In 1952 he was sentenced to ten years after a man was killed in Carlton.

His record included assaults, robberies and thefts.

In 1971 he was shot outside his home in Orr Street, Carlton. The gunman leaned over the bonnet of a parked car and said, 'Where do you want it, Morris?' before blasting him with a shotgun in the leg.

Morris drove himself to St Vincent's Hospital for treatment.

In 1973, on his 39th wedding anniversary, he went to the local pub for a drink and told his wife, 'If I'm not back in an hour you will find me in the morgue.'

Later that night he was arrested for being drunk and died within hours in the South Melbourne lock-up. He was 58.

Over the years Morris had drunk himself to death. The then Assistant Commissioner for Crime, Bill Crowley said: 'All senior police knew Horatio. He was one of the toughest criminals I have known.'

In his later years Morris befriended a young man and guided him into the criminal world. He helped turn Chopper Read from just another violent street fighter into one of the most dangerous criminals in the country.

Read saw him as an underworld father figure and was eager to learn from his experience. In return Horatio was able to rely on the physical strength of Read to protect him as his own power withered.

Old Horatio Morris taught me one important lesson: that a man's enemy is his greatest teacher. Horatio was an old-time lone-wolf gunman. I'm proud to say he was a good friend – and he taught me some valuable lessons. He taught me who was who in Melbourne, and who to worry about. The only person to really worry about, he told me, was myself – because 'gun against gun' evens everything up.

Horatio had faced them all down. Fred Harrison, Norm Bradshaw – even my old friend Billy Longley – would not go out of their way to upset old Horatio. He was by no means a big money crime figure, but he would put a bullet in you at the proverbial drop of a hat – and in a gun battle he was a dead shot.

I have a .22 calibre bullet hole in the left side of my back. Horatio's girlfriend, the former lady friend of the late Norman Bradshaw, a lady in her 40s in 1972 or 1973, shot me in the back 'by accident' with her little five-shot-single action American .22 handgun. She was a bit drunk at the time and 'terribly sorry'.

Cowboy John Harris dug the slug out with a pocket knife, and he made a right pig's breakfast of it, I must say.

Horatio Morris once said to me: 'Never grow to love anybody too much, because one day you might have to kill them.' I never forgot that, and that motto has kept me alive. It also meant I knew where I stood with Horatio. We liked each other, and he liked my company, and we would go out together regularly until his death in early 1973. He was a very, very ill man in his last days, going a bit blind and an alcoholic. I liked him – but I never, ever trusted him. He taught me a great deal but his motto shook me to the bone. His outlook on life and people was harder than mine could ever be. I needed his old brain to teach me. He needed my strength to throw his punches.

Horatio was a great one for shooting battles behind the bar in pubs, and was still picking up several hundred dollars a week from SP bookies in South Melbourne before he died.

I could never really pick his age. He looked about 100 to me. Alcohol had pickled him. He was from the era of gun-carrying drunks – instead of the knife-carrying HIV-positive junkies that roam the streets of Melbourne today.

Horatio was a great one for the races, and we had some good days at the track together. We met some interesting people. Every crim in Melbourne, half the coppers and most of the judges, barristers and TV stars – the posh from the south and the rough from the west – all mixing together, all friendly on the racetrack.

In the carpark at Caulfield one day I walked into one of Australia's top judges taking a leak. He didn't know me, but he knew Horatio Morris. Horatio said: 'Put it away, or you'll get us all pinched.' There was great laughter. The races are good like that.

A great knockabout, quiet and polite little gentleman was old Tommy Woodcock. I met him at the Caulfield and Melbourne Cups. I also met Derek Nimmo, although that's no big deal. A few drinks and anyone can meet Derek Nimmo at the races.

Me and Horatio were standing, waiting to put on a bet. We had Lillian Frank in front of us talking to Andrew Peacock, Charlie Wootton standing in front of them, Tommy

Woodcock talking to Horatio Morris, and behind us was Derek Nimmo talking to the TV star Abigail. The races are a true comical melting pot. Gang wars, political wars and all problems and troubles get left at the gate. I love the races, and the races in Melbourne are the best of all.

At one Melbourne Cup – I think it was about 1972 – Horatio introduced me to a well-known Brighton socialite, a very horny-looking blonde who's always in the papers. Horatio didn't even know the lady personally but she was talking to Jack Paccholi. Horatio walked up and said: 'Piss off, Jack,' and Paccholi couldn't get away quick enough. Then old Horatio started: 'Dear lady, I thought I'd rescue you from the foul clutches of that gangster of the gutter press.' She giggled. Then he said: 'Let me introduce myself and my young, thuggish-looking companion. I am Horatio Morris of the Port Melbourne Morrises, and this is Chopper Read of the Thomastown Reads. Now, if you would be kind enough to escort us to the Members' Car Park, I'll allow you to buy us some champagne.' She giggled some more and said, 'I don't think my husband would like that.'

Horatio said: 'Then, my darling girl, this way up to the bar,' and off we went. I left Horatio to it. He could be an old smoothie with the ladies. I often wonder whether she polished his gun. But Horatio was an old gent. He wouldn't kiss and tell, so I don't know how he went ... and I'm damn sure the lady won't be telling anyone.

In the early 1970s I used to love gatecrashing other people's parties. The night after the Melbourne Cup was the best time of the year. One year, me, Dave the Jew, Cowboy Johnny Harris, Terry Tempest and a dead drunk Horatio Morris gatecrashed a very swank affair – very posh – in Kew, I think. It was a house owned by Prue Acton and her husband Mr Mike Treloar. No one even knew we were gatecrashers – the house was half-full of other gatecrashers.

Prue Acton and Mike Treloar wouldn't remember me, but I remember the night well. There was a Miss Australia there who was as pissed as a parrot – and more than friendly with all the boys.

It was the first time I'd tasted Veuve Clicquot champagne.

A GREAT DAY

Kings, Queens, Knockabouts and crooks,
All in together,
Like a yard full of chooks,
The South Yarra ladies,
Out for a fling,
Getting dated by the roughnecks,
As they stand in the betting ring,
The fallen and the famous,
The wealthy and the poor,
All betting money,
And counting up their score,

Everyone's relaxed,
No need to watch your back
She's a bloody great day,
At the Caulfield racing track.

Barry Quinn

Barry Robert Quinn was convicted of the double murder of two men during the armed robbery of the Car-O-Tel Motel in St Kilda in 1974.

He escaped from the Fairfield Infectious Disease Hospital in 1978 where he was being treated for suspected hepatitis. In the 69 days he was at large five people associated with him were murdered. They were Eve Karlson, Wayne Smith, Sheryl Anne Gardner and her nine-year-old son, Danny William Mitchell, and Lisa Maude Brearley.

Quinn, with his long hair and history of violence, became known as Australia's Charles Manson. He was later killed in Jika Jika by fellow inmate Alex Tsakmakis, who burned him alive on July 5, 1984. Quinn got out of his league and started to bait Tsakmakis in Jika Jika about the rape of his girlfriend.

After watching a video Quinn continued to yell insults to Tsakmakis. The next day Tsakmakis pounced, pouring model glue over Quinn and then flicking lit matches at the inmate. He caught fire and was injured fatally.

But even in hospital before he died Quinn observed the code and refused to tell police the name of the man who had set him on fire, although there was no doubt it was Tsakmakis.

When told by police he was going to die he replied, 'Yeah, I know. So what's the drama?'

In relation to Barry Quinn, unlike a lot of people I didn't like the little numbskull. He was a coward, a liar, junkie and a jail cat, slang meaning he indulged in homosexual conduct behind prison walls. He had a longstanding love affair with a famous, now dead, Pentridge drag queen, Rhonda Rock Jaw, when the two of them were in B Division in 1975–76.

I would describe Quinn's death as one of the more welcome fires Pentridge has had, and if Tsakmakis could be remembered for anything even closely resembling an act of Christian decency, then putting an end to Quinn would be it.

In relation to his first murders, the Car-O-Tel job, everyone who knew the men involved knew he didn't pull the trigger, even though he bragged he did. The guys who did used to laugh behind his back. He had a bloated sense of who he was and how he wanted others to see him. He bragged of being a Painter and Docker. Whether he held a docky's brief, who knows, but he did hang around with dockies.

No matter what could be said about his crimes and his so-called violence and his heavy crimes, he was, in reality, a weak-gutted thing. He couldn't punch his way out of a poofters' tea party. I would describe him as a lace hankie with a Charles Manson fixation. He only attacked when he felt he was backed up by the pack. On the day he died he felt he had the numbers and he was, no doubt, in a state of total mental collapse to think he could try Alex on for size and survive the encounter. I mean, what more can I say. As for his murders, it was hardly the streets of Tombstone, Main Street at high noon.

It was square heads, women and kids, that sort of thing. The only thing he had in common with the Kelly gang was his beard and whiskers. His was cowardly violence of a mindless nature directed against the weak, without courage, style or flair.

Whatever Tsakmakis was or was not, he did have a sense of style. Quinn was totally without style. If you were to set up quality control on acts of violence and murder then you would have to call Quinn a total retard. The only act of real stylish violence Quinn ever took part in was his own death. The only real true love he had in his life was a prostitute called Eve. Quinn had the words Eve tattooed all over his hands, feet and body. I believe he later was involved in her murder after he escaped in 1978.

He wasn't any deep, dark complex master murderer, he was a two-bob cheap little arse wipe.

Garry David

Garry David is the criminal who forced the Victorian Government to enact special legislation to keep him in jail.

He is a psychopath, a self-mutilator and, according to police, one of the most dangerous men in Australia.

He has cut off his ears, nipples and penis as well as eating razor blades and glass. He has spent most of his life in institutions.

He was due to be released from Pentridge in 1990 after serving a sentence for shooting a policeman and a shop owner in Rye.

While in jail he threatened to make the mass murder of Hoddle Street 'look like a picnic'.

He has repeatedly made threats that he would murder people on his release.

The Government passed the Community Protection Act to keep David in jail after he had completed his jail term as he was considered a danger to society.

I've known Garry David 'Webb' since I was 20. He is related to a well-known and respected Melbourne business family. The wrong side of the family, it would seem. I knew one of his relatives who spent most of his life in jail. He was a bisexual and a sexual pervert.

When Garry was 16 or 17 he found himself, don't ask me how, in C Division, and the relative chased Garry with a knife, trying to have sex with him. The old bloke is dead now.

My old dad used to say to me that we complain about having no shoes until we see a man with no feet. If I was born with no shoes, Garry was born with no feet. From what he has told me of his childhood, mine was a happy one by comparison.

In our younger days Garry looked up to me and did me a lot of good turns. I would not allow the homosexual elements within jail to pick on Garry, as he had been attacked in boys' homes as a small kid and in jails as a 17- and 18-year-old.

I feel guilty about Garry, as he cut his ears off after I did and then he went one better and cut part of his private parts off. I wrote to him and said, 'Garry, I am no longer the head of the Van Gogh Club in Pentridge. You are. When the dickie birds start dropping to the pavement, that's enough for me. I might be mad, but I'm not stupid.'

I don't feel sorry for many men, but Garry's hopeless situation makes me feel sorry. His life seems to have no answers. He is not a friend, but we have been friendly.

He was given a piece of a large estate when a relative died. He gave it to people who he thought had less than he had. I wonder who they were.

Garry David is not a real criminal. He is just another sad and lost soul in the sewer of hell. Is he dangerous? Physically, not at all. Mentally, yes. But considering his life, whose fault is it?

Joe Ditroia

Joe 'The Boss' Ditroia was one of Read's main allies inside H Division. Like most of Read's friends he was no stranger to violence. Between crimes he was a cleaner and a pizza maker. He has been involved in assaults, escapes, firearm offences and armed robberies.

'Joe the Boss' Ditroia is a top man with a knife. For anyone who has seen the movie *Goodfellas*, the Tommy character played by Academy-Award winning actor Joe Pesci is a dead ringer for Joe the Boss.

Joe is a South Australian Italian, and is doing time now in Yatala Prison. He found it hard to stay out of trouble, but he and his family have shown me great kindness and friendship.

Joe was Alex Tsakmakis's arch enemy on the card table, as he acted as boss of the manila table. No matter who he played Joe was never beaten at cards. That's how he got the name 'Joe The Boss'. Joe was my right-hand man in H Division in 1988 and 1989.

He was acquitted in court over the ice-pick stabbing of Melbourne underworld figure and massage parlour boss Sandy Macrae. Joe was acquitted on grounds of self-defence. Some unkind people, including Macrae, hinted that I ordered the stabbing. However, this is yet another case of 'foul slander and gossip'.

A court of law found that poor Joe the Boss was the victim of a cowardly attack – and replied to the attack by planting an ice pick into Macrae's back twice. I should know: I was a witness. And let me tell you, it was a clear-cut case of self-defence.

JOE THE BOSS

From South Australia, came a fellow,
With an Italian temper, hardly mellow,
With gun in hand, he was quite quick,
He'd put one in you, nice and slick,
And with a blade, he was very handy,

> *Just ask a Melbourne hoon named Sandy,*
> *But cards he loved to play,*
> *He'd beat the boys every day,*
> *Yes, with a deck of cards, he was never at a loss,*
> *The King of the table, Joe the Boss.*

Michael Ebert

Michael Ebert was a man with a reputation. A convicted killer, Ebert was a high roller in the Melbourne massage parlour scene. Ebert, Keith George Faure and Hans George Obrenovic were found guilty of manslaughter over the killing of Shane Dennis 'Jock' Rowland, who was gunned down in a North Fitzroy house in May 1976.

Ebert was sentenced to eight years but was out in three. Within days of being released he was back to his trade and was soon making $1,000 running three parlours.

On April 17, 1980, he was shot dead outside one of his parlours in Rathdowne Street, Carlton. His murder has never been solved.

In 1974 I bashed and nearly kicked to death a young, up and coming standover man, gunman and so-called heavy as he walked out of the Retreat Hotel in Collingwood, Mick Ebert.

Yet somehow this pussy maintained a heavy and feared reputation within the Melbourne underworld until his death.

He was, to my way of thinking, only a two-bob pimp and he had never fought or beaten anyone of any real importance within the Melbourne criminal world. How this arse wipe ever got his reputation is beyond my power of understanding. When he came to jail in the mid 1970s he acted as bodyguard to my old enemy, Keith Faure, until he realised that Faure expected him to fight against me and then Ebert and Faure fell out and Ebert vanished into the mainstream of the prison system, leaving poor Keithy to wage war alone.

I must say that I ended up respecting Keithy Faure as during the five or so years of gang wars between us he took a terrible beating and defeat after defeat, yet he did have blind guts. He lacked tactics and strategies, and was betrayed and left like a shag on a rock by many of his so-called close personal friends, yet he never surrendered. I respected his blind courage.

Danny McIntosh

Danny Francis McIntosh was a major armed robber and an accomplished truck hijacker. He was involved in breaking and entering. He had a reputation as a man who could always get a hand on a gun. McIntosh was well respected by criminals as a professional armed robber who always did his homework before a big job. But while crime was his job, according to Read, buxom, famous women were his obsession.

There was a real good little bank robber called Danny McIntosh who later died of leukaemia. I used to bump into him in pubs and clubs as well as in jail in the 1970s and 80s. As well as his involvement in massive criminal concerns he had a funny side.

He was always falling in love with television stars and making outrageous fairytale plans to kidnap them. He started with Princess Panda in the 1960s, so I'm told, and then he got excited over Cheryl Rixon in the 1970s, then Abigail. But his greatest moment was his plot to kidnap Lynda Stoner in 1977. Meetings were called and plots hatched for real. He even approached me as none of his bank robbery mates would have a bar of it.

Danny cornered me in the South Yarra Arms in 1977. He told me he had a private detective, Tom Ericksen, follow Lynda so he knew her address in Melbourne and where her relatives lived in South Australia. He had photos taken of her and even knew where she did her shopping. He was really quite nutty over her.

He certainly did his homework on her. There is no doubt he wanted to have her abducted. He wanted me to do the actual kidnapping because he didn't want Lynda to be frightened of him. His plan was that he wanted to 'save' her. He was to come to the hideout and in front of her he was going to talk me out of it and then take her to safety. I was supposed to wear a balaclava.

He told me he wanted me to abduct her at gunpoint and not to be too gentle about it. I was to take her to a secret location for about two days.

Danny imagined that would be long enough to break her will.

All this was to be done in an attempt to impress Ms Stoner

who would then fall head over heels for Danny.

Danny was a sex maniac. He was very cool when it came to robbing banks, but on anything else he was loopy. He always gave me the impression that he was under the influence of some mind-altering drugs.

I have no doubt that he wanted to go ahead with the plan. I have no idea what would have happened to the girl if she had resisted his advances.

Suffice to say it would probably not be wise to get involved with a drug-crazed armed robber who thought he loved you.

He was not a big man, in fact he was a bit of a weed. But he carried a gun and was crazy.

Anything could have happened if the plan went ahead.

Lynda Stoner was not well known then. I think she had just started to appear on television and her picture had been in a few magazines, but it was enough that Danny got a crush on her.

I said, 'Danny, we'll all get 100 years jail for this, for Christ's sake. Send the bloody woman some flowers instead.' I believe that in the end he did send her some flowers 'from a secret admirer'.

Yes, Danny was a very weird little man, in regard to his personal thinking. He was one of a group of crims who used the drug LSD in the 60s.

They were all the same. They had that sort of spaced-out thinking process. You know, there was a little bit of Charles Manson about him.

Danny was a little runt of a bloke but he was deadly serious about his plans with Ms Stoner. Meetings were held and plans were made. He was quite crackers about her.

I don't think anyone had the heart to tell him that Ms Stoner would probably have been able to beat him in a fist fight. If she had got her arms free after she was tied up, I think Danny would have been in trouble.

Danny was always good to me. A grand in my hand whenever I saw him. He was no fool.

Lenny Knape

Leonard Allan Knape was an armed robber who learnt first hand that crime doesn't always pay. On February 3, 1978, Knape, with partner, Stanley Robert Walters robbed the Reservoir Target Supermarket of $12,000. In the car park they were confronted by an off-duty armed robbery squad detective, Brendan Bannan. Shots were exchanged and Knape ended up with a bullet in the chest and Walters one in the stomach. Knape was later sentenced to 14 years jail.

Lenny Knape was a top bank robber and gunman and one of the best standup street fighters in Pentridge. He gave it to Bill O'Meally in H Division in the 1960s. That was back in the days when O'Meally ran H Division.

Lenny was only a young chap then. I first met Lenny in Bendigo Prison back in 1986; he was very kind to me and one of the true gentlemen I have met in my life.

He was shot in the shoulder during an armed robbery by a well-known and now high-ranking policeman, Brendan Bannan.

Later, Lenny got married, got out of jail in 1986 shortly before I did and I believe he got involved in the church. He was involved in social welfare work, helping released prisoners in some sort of half-way house set-up. He hasn't been back to jail and I can only wish him all the very best. Before he left jail I said, 'Come in with me, Lenny, and we'll get into the toe-cutting business.'

He laughed, patted me on the shoulder and said, 'Ten years ago, Chopper, when I was younger and madder, maybe. But I want to get out and live, not get out and die.'

All I can say is, we would have had a top time together. But, then again, maybe I should have listened to him.

Joey Hamilton

Joey Hamilton was a man who liked to talk. He talked to the Beach Inquiry into the Police. He talked to politicians. He talked to reporters and he talked to other criminals. He was charged and convicted over an armed robbery in 1973, but the conviction was later quashed. He received $26,000 in compensation for his time in prison.

Joey Hamilton, or Mangles as he was called, was one of the most boring individuals I'd ever come across in jail. If I hadn't already cut my ears off; I'm sure he would have tried to talk them off. I knew him in B Division in 1975. Jimmy Loughnan and I had an escape plan, for me it was my one and only escape attempt, but for Jimmy it was plan 300.

Don't ask me how, but Joey Hamilton got his head in on the action. All I ever wanted to do with his head was push it down a toilet bowl. I found him to be a chatterbox.

But another bloke thought well of him and so did Jimmy so he was in. Well, on the big day I was there with 60 feet of rope and a tomahawk, Jimmy had some rope and a big knife and the other bloke arrived to say that Joey wasn't coming because there was a good show on TV. He had just got a new television set in his cell. I started towards his cell but ended up laughing about it rather than killing him. I have never forgotten Hamilton, a true man of steel.

Some time later Jimmy decided he didn't like Joey. He got it into his head that we should have a game of cricket in the B Division yard and use Hamilton's head as the cricket ball. He wanted us to cut his head off for the game.

I must say that Jimmy could flip right out now and again and he was a very dangerous man. Joey was as nice as pie to both of us, he always was well mannered and eager to chat. He just gave me the shits.

Well, Jimmy found out that Ray Chuck, who was Jimmy's hero, didn't like Joey, and that was enough to start Loughnan stewing and brooding.

Jimmy Loughnan was a good mate of Jockey Smith. Jimmy loved robbing banks. He was a useless bank robber, a total failure, but he was a massive trier. When Ray Chuck said he didn't like Hamilton, that was it for Jimmy.

The cricket game with Hamilton's head as the cricket ball was more than just a fantasy; Jim was quite serious. I was happy with the idea of wasting Hamilton, any excuse was better than none, but Jimmy's idea of the cricket game meant a certain life sentence.

Killing Hamilton wasn't the issue, doing a life sentence for it was. Luckily, for all of us, especially Hamilton, I managed to talk Jimmy out of the idea. Jimmy was as mad as a hatter, poor bugger.

Scottish Steve

The Speed King of Melbourne's western suburbs is a man known as 'Scottish Steve', and he is the greatest threat to the Lygon Street Crew. He once thought I was part of a plot to kill him, but that was not true.

Scottish Steve is a man of average height and weight, but fit and strong. With his black hair and moustache he looks more like a Sicilian than a Scot. He is a martial arts expert, a master with samurai swords, a marksman and a gun collector.

He carries a 9mm handgun or a .38 automatic at all times, reputedly sleeping with one under the pillow. He also has a semi-automatic rifle beside his bed.

Steve either controls or stands over most of the speed in the western suburbs.

He is protected by various electronic alarm systems, booby

traps and two German Shepherd guard dogs. He is an art collector, and many believe he has in his possession a painting by Goya, stolen of course.

Scottish Steve uses speed himself and the massive paranoia from that habit mixed with a mild mental condition and his morbid and unhealthy interest in the mystic arts and black magic makes him one of the strangest men I have ever met.

He once told a group of us that when it rained he didn't get wet. He was convinced that he had special mystical powers. He used to sit in his backyard in full martial arts uniform, on a Japanese white rug with his samurai swords and assorted weapons around him. He would have the incense burning and he would drink a mixture of his and his German Shepherd's blood while putting curses of death on his assorted enemies.

The man is a dangerous nut. I once acted as a bodyguard for him over a short period of time while he was having bother with the Lygon Street crew. He paid big dollars but he was crippled with a paranoid mental condition which had him running around inside his house with a rifle, convinced that two well-known Melbourne detectives were in the house across the road, and the father of one of the detectives was mowing the lawn.

Steve was a mental case. He would test fire his guns in the backyard and when he got arrested he couldn't work out how the police got on to him – never thinking for a moment that it could have been his fault.

I once caught Steve naked in his backyard cleaning his two

German Shepherds with a vacuum cleaner. He claimed the vacuum cleaner picked up all the fleas.

Steve is out and about now and he has been for some time and, I am reliably informed, as nutty as ever. He is still convinced that with his mystical powers and Satan's help he and his small army of speed-ravaged nutcases will fight the good fight against the forces of darkness. I like Steve and will not put his last name in this. Any enemy of the Carlton Crew is a mate of mine, regardless of insanity. There are some weird and wonderful chaps running around out there but Sottish Steve is one of the weirdest, believe me.

Steve sees Lygon Street and the Fairy Godfather as, to quote Steve himself, 'the head of the snake which must be destroyed'.

As a matter of interest, Steve used to put two teaspoons of speed into his dogs' water dish. No wonder they were the craziest German Shepherds in Melbourne.

Nick Apostolidis

Nick Apostolidis was a drug dealer who wishes he had never heard the name Chopper Read.

The former car salesman, butcher and fork-lift driver who has prior convictions for rape, obscene exposure, drug trafficking, robbery and carrying a firearm learnt first-hand from Read what it was like to be the hunted rather than the hunter.

He didn't like it.

Read shot Apostolidis's friend Chris Liapis in the stomach then told the injured man, 'Justice comes out of the end of a barrel.' Read later burnt Apostolidis's house down. He also fired shots in Apostolidis's mother's home in 1987 during a campaign of terror.

Now Nick The Greek is not what you would call a heavy criminal. He is, in fact, a nitwit.

He was a western suburbs drug dealer. Sure I burnt his house down, so what? As I said to him later when I was asked why I burnt it down: 'I love a sunburnt country.'

Who would make a fuss about burning his house down? I know I got two years jail for that and shooting the drug dealer. So what? Burning Nick the Greek's house down, big deal, who cares? Don't mention to me about old Nick the Greek, with his $60,000 a month out of heroin and wanting to whinge to me about the burning down of his house. He's only screaming because he lost his dope in the house.

You may think I was a little cruel firing shots at his mother's house but the truth is I think that Nick should thank me for what I have done for him. Being my enemy has launched some formerly unknown criminals into the criminal world's version of superstars. It's quite amusing.

Nick is a prime example. Before I burnt his house down and shot up his mum's home it was a case of Nick the Greek Who? Now he is a criminal superstar.

You might think I treated him a little harshly, but look at it this way. When Nick's grandchildren sit at his feet and say, 'What did you do in the old days, Grandad?' he can say to them with pride, 'Chopper Read burnt my house down.' There we have the sum total of Nick the Greek's claim to fame. God save us all.

People who ask me why I burnt his house down obviously don't know Nick. Any reasonable person who met him would either want to knock him out or burn his house down. He is an obnoxious character who really can't kick a goal.

On reflection, I believe that Nick the Greek should be set on fire himself on a regular basis. As a street fighter he would make a great ladies' hairdresser. In the world of real criminals Nick is not noted for his bravery.

Look at his working history, he has been a car salesman and a drug dealer. I wouldn't buy a vehicle from him, unless it was a used fire truck.

A short postscript to me burning down Nick the Greek's house in Footscray. Every Christmas since then I have sent him a Christmas card and on it I write.

'Dear Nick,
I shook your nerves and I rattled your brain,
My kind of love just drove you insane,
I broke your will,
Oh what a thrill,
Goodness gracious great balls of fire,
Ha Ha,
Thinking of you always, Chopper.'

Paul Steven Haig and Robert Wright

Paul Steven Haig is one of the most notorious convicted mass murderers in Australia. He has admitted to killing six people in an 11-month period. His victims include women and a nine-year-old boy.

Haig killed Caulfield pizza-shop owner Bruno Cingolani on December 7, 1978, spinster Evelyn Abrahams at the Prahran Tattersalls agency where she worked on September 21, 1978, criminal Wayne Keith Smith on June 27, 1979, Sheryl Anne Gardener and her son, Danny William Mitchell, on July 22, 1979, and was involved in the murder of Eve Karlson. He is serving six life sentences for the murders plus 15 years for robberies and malicious wounding. He says that he has now changed and no longer considers himself a criminal.

During the murder spree he teamed up with Robert Wright, who was also convicted over multiple murders.

Wright had a history of escaping from jail. He was one of the most violent men in the jail. Wright was one of the five prison inmates who died in the Jika Jika division fire in 1987.

He was considered to be the ringleader of the group and the man who had the idea to start the fire as a protest. He was furious because his application to be moved from Jika had been rejected. The plan was to start the fire to destroy the unit. The men underestimated the density of the smoke and were overcome and died before prison officers could get to them.

I knew Haig on the outside in the sharpie days of the 1970s.

He was always a quiet sort of fellow, very meek and non-violent. His friendship with Robert Wright was odd but not homosexual. Haig stated in court once he was a homosexual but he wasn't. Why he would want to claim that he was a homosexual was a puzzle. If he walked into a gay liberation meeting they would call the police. He teamed up with Wright for a while but Robert ended up hating him.

If Wright hadn't died in the Jika Jika fire I think he would have ended up killing Haig. Wright used to joke that if Haig tried to earn his living as a male prostitute he would have died of starvation. He is not, and never has been a homosexual.

Wright told me that Haig once read a book on an American psychopath mass killer who was homosexual and maybe Haig thought that was a good image to have. And as for his newfound love of God – the number of nutters in jail who give their hearts to God is frightening. I certainly wouldn't want to kneel for a quiet word of prayer in front of that congregation, let me tell you.

Wright told me that Haig's new Christian feelings were about as real as his homosexuality. Anyone thinking that Haig is just a Bible-bashing poofter is making a big mistake. If a homosexual priest went to Haig with the offer of some activity in the shower room he would be a dead man. If Jack the Ripper met Haig on a dark night, Jack would shit himself.

I knew Bobby Wright since we were both young blokes in Prahran. Mad Charlie told me he used to stand over Wright for his lunch money at Prahran Tech. I used to love to tease

him about that, even though I was never sure if it was true. I
left school at 15 and never went to Prahran Tech. But we got
around a few pool rooms together, knocked about now and
again as young guys, not real friends, just now and again
knockabout mates.

Robert wasn't half as mad as people thought. He'd act a bit
psycho to get people going and he wasn't any sort of a fighter.
In fact, poor Robert couldn't beat time with a bass drum. I
don't know, to others he was a psychopathic killer, but when
you've known a guy since he was a kid, you see him in a
different light. My old dad still carries a handmade leather
wallet with KEITH engraved into the leather that Robert
Wright made for him.

One thing people outside Pentridge don't know. Robert
Wright was without a shadow of doubt the finest chess player
in the prison system. Totally unbeatable among the prisoners
and staff who challenged him.

I beat Robert in six moves once, but I had a bit of a
psychological advantage ... I was carrying a tomahawk at the
time. I'm sure Robert let me win to be on the safe side. Ha,
ha.

Robert and Jimmy Loughnan were known as Heckle and
Jeckle, but the crazy psycho act was just that.

Craig Minogue was on the other side of the unit when it
went up. He nearly died as well. What can anyone really say.

Jimmy Loughnan and Robert Wright cut the throat of and
nearly killed Sydney crim Colin Stratton in Jika Jika. Stratton

had pistol-whipped Robert's sister.

Frankie Waghorn

Frankie Waghorn is considered one of the toughest men in prison. He was found guilty and then granted a re-trial over the stabbing murder of John Turner. In 1991 he stood trial again and was convicted of the murder.

If there is anyone around who can throw a punch harder than Frankie Waghorn, I haven't met him.

We have been friends without cross words for some 20 years. The only time it came close to bloodshed, and this is something Frankie doesn't even know, was after his fight with Mad Charlie in B Division in 1975. Afterwards I asked Charlie if he wanted revenge, and revenge would have meant big bloodshed. Frankie was, and still is, a respected and feared criminal identity, and bloodshed against Frank would have started a gang war inside Pentridge that would have moved to the streets after release.

Frankie Waghorn would punch the false teeth out of an elephant. Charlie, when faced with real life-and-death blood and guts, preferred to take a low profile and shake hands. In a way I'm glad Frankie Waghorn is a good friend.

Frankie was arrested for the murder of Johnny Turner in 1989. Turner was the beloved nephew of old-time gangster and underworld figure, Joseph Patrick Turner. Rumours of revenge soon turned to handshakes when Frankie Waghorn walked into the Jika Jika hotel in Fitzroy. Old Joey didn't want a war. A war with Waghorn also meant a war with me, and whatever else I may do badly, I don't lose gang wars. While other kids were playing marbles, I was playing war, and reading military history.

I am personally convinced Frank didn't kill Johnny Turner. Frank wouldn't need a knife to kill anyone. He punches so hard he would have punched Turner into the wall and left him there as an air vent.

Frankie Waghorn is a pretty good jailhouse cook. However, he is nowhere near Slim Minogue's standard.

When Frankie first started to cook for me I was convinced he thought that Cordon Bleu was a French bank robber.

He could have received 10 with a 7-year minimum for any dish he made but through trial and error he ended up doing a fantastic fried rice, with smoked oysters, capsicums, onions, garlic, paprika, egg, and assorted spice which would have gone down well at The Flower Drum Chinese Restaurant.

The trouble was that Frankie only knew how to cook fried rice. If you eat fried rice seven days a week, it can get on your nerves, so he tried Italian stew. Frankie is no Italian and for a moment there I thought it was a plot to kill me. But he improved on that with spaghetti, meat balls, garlic, paprika, onions, capsicums and HP sauce. Very tasty.

Now and again we wash it down with a nice bottle of el cheapo plonk, a red or white, or the odd drop of Dimple

Scotch whisky. Well, if the junkies can get their stuff in, I see no reason why I should go without.

Keith Faure

Keith George Faure is a murderer, armed robber and a career criminal who is considered one of the major players in the Victorian underworld. He was the criminal who stood against Read in the Pentridge civil war which went for more than five years.

Faure has been convicted of two manslaughters, armed robbery and the shooting of a policeman.

He was convicted of shooting Senior-Constable Michael Pratt in the back during the robbery of an ANZ bank in Clifton Hill on June 4, 1976.

Faure shot Pratt as the off-duty policeman tried to stop the robbery.

Pratt received the George Cross for bravery but was forced to retire because of his injuries.

He was convicted of killing Shane Dennis Rowland in a Richmond house on May 1, 1976.

He was also convicted of the November 1976 killing of fellow Pentridge inmate Alan Sopulak, who was stabbed nine times with a sharpened butter knife.

Faure was first charged with breaking and entering when he was 11. He has a history of escape, theft and violence.

He gives his occupations as Painter and Docker, slaughterman and abalone sheller.

Within weeks of being released early from jail in late 1987 he was involved in the armed robbery of a Thornbury jewellery shop which left a man dead. Faure was sentenced to 13 years for his involvement.

In 1990 he was stabbed twice in the chest in Pentridge's B Division.

His wife, Sandra, lived with armed robber, Graeme Jensen, who was killed by police in 1988.

Faure broke the long-standing underworld code and made a statement to police after the killing. He claimed to know that Jensen was carrying a gun at the time he was killed.

He said Jensen had to carry a gun because he was afraid that Faure's friends would kill him for living with Sandra.

Faure later repudiated the statement to the Coronial Inquest.

But criminals have long memories and according to Read, Faure's statement to the police has left him a marked man.

I think that before too long there will be a major underworld war as a result of a statement made by police to Keith Faure.

Keithy went against the Walsh Street crew in an under-the-counter manner that now has been found out. This will only end when Keithy is killed or a gang war will break out on his release.

Keithy was once an enemy of mine so this one will be interesting to watch. The Carlton Crew have also been sent a copy of Keithy's statement as they have backed him for years. Faure has little or no support left in the criminal world, but if this came down to a battle of the streets I wouldn't discount him for one second. It should be a nice old bloodbath either way. Neither side is what I would call heavy thinkers regarding tactics and in the world of blood and guts, gun against gun, I would describe both sides as a total comedy of errors. Keithy Faure was once a power of sorts in the criminal world, but this has finished him. Even if he wins the physical battle, he is finished.

I am pleased to say that this will be one shit fight in Melbourne that does not involve my good self, however I am looking forward to some high comedy as a result of it. What's life without a giggle. Personally, I wouldn't take either side to a shit fight on a dark night.

Amos Atkinson

One of the original members of the Overcoat Gang and a man with a taste for gang war almost equal to Chopper's was Amos Atkinson.

From the age of 12 he wanted to be a gangster. He used to have pictures of Al Capone stuck on his bedroom walls.

He was expelled from school when he went to classes drunk at the age of 13 and soon graduated to stealing cars. By the age of 18 he was serving eight years in Pentridge for armed robbery.

He teamed up with Read and took part in a war which raged behind the walls of Pentridge for five years.

In 1979 he cut off his ears to become a member of the Van Gogh Club in Pentridge a year after Read lost his own.

In 1978 Atkinson held 30 people hostage at gunpoint in a Melbourne restaurant, The Italian Waiters' Club, in a failed bid to have Read released from jail.

Atkinson said that if Read was not released within 24 hours he would begin to kill hostages. The siege failed after four hours and Atkinson was arrested. Atkinson fired shots at police during a wild cab ride outside the club before the siege began.

He was convicted and sentenced to five years for the offences.

But Read and Atkinson were later to fall out. Read said Atkinson failed to warn him he had been earmarked to be killed in a knife attack inside H Division.

Read no longer considers Atkinson an ally.

I suspect that Amos Atkinson started to dislike me way back in the early 1980s in Jika Jika. He was in unit two, side two and I was in unit two, side one.

Amos had been sent a beautiful electric clock radio; he went out to sign for it and took it out of the box. I was standing at the glass doorway watching. Amos had a look of almost childlike wonder on his face, he was so delighted with the new clock radio. I yelled out in front of the screws, 'Amos, white man make big magic in little box. Ha ha.'

Amos smashed the lovely clock radio on the cement floor and went to his cell, the bloody sook. Some people just can't take a joke.

When I got out of jail in November 1986, I found Amos living in a de facto relationship with a white girl. She was a nice enough young lass, but I found the relationship distasteful. In the wee hours of the morning in 1987 I pulled up outside

Amos's house, blind drunk, stood on the front lawn and let off three shots to awaken the household. Then, at the top of my voice I proceeded to sing that old country and western classic:

'Oh there's one thing I can't figure and that's a white girl with a nigger.'

Amos yelled out the window, 'Piss off, you mad bastard' and I ran to my car and sped off; firing shots in the air, laughing my head off as I went.

I suspect the rot set into the friendship after that.

Amos was not amused. I, however, felt it was the very height of good humour.

At one stage I planned to stuff Amos head–first into a tree shredder but I decided against it. I hope that one day I don't regret my Christian kindness.

Billy Longley

Painter and Docker, Billy 'The Texan' Longley, was one of the hard men who ran the Melbourne docks when the docks were the centre of the underworld.

In 1971 he stood for election as President of the Victorian branch of the union. The election was held and Longley was confident he had won, but a short time later the ballot box was stolen and there was a fire in the office.

When the result was announced it was Arthur Morris who was elected President.

The secretary of the union, Pat Shannon, was gunned down in the bar of the Druids Hotel in South Melbourne, on October 17, 1973.

The Texan was charged with the murder. The Crown alleged that he paid another man, Kevin Taylor, $6,000 to kill Shannon.

Longley served 13 years for the murder, always claiming he was innocent. Shannon was a popular man and from the day of the murder The Texan had to mind his back.

Longley was no stranger to courts. He had been charged with the murder of his first wife, Patricia, in 1961. He was found guilty of manslaughter but was later acquitted on appeal.

Allegations of organised crime and corruption made by Longley to The Bulletin *magazine resulted in the then Prime Minister, Malcolm Fraser, setting up the Costigan Royal Commission.*

Longley told the Commission that since 1958 between 30 and 40 Painters and Dockers had been murdered as part of a union civil war.

Longley broke the traditional Painters and Dockers code of silence. Many police believed Longley would be killed by union supporters. But Read decided he would protect, and if need be kill for, The Texan.

In the years Longley served for the murder of Shannon, no enemy got past Read to complete the act of revenge. Longley was released in 1988.

But while Longley has left the scene there are many criminals who still hate Read because he stood between them and the man they call 'The Texan.'

My friendship with The Texan started as an odd one. Some of the plots and plans that we put together in the late 70s I could never write about. Let's just say that Putty Nose Nicholls and

Bobby Dix weren't on our Christmas list. Had I been supplied with the weapons as promised in 1976, then when I got out in 1977, the Victorian Branch of the Federated Ship Painters and Dockers would have drowned in a sea of their own blood and I would not have supplied lifeboats for the women and kids.

I was told to contact a chap re fully automatic weapons, but the party I was told to contact lost his guts, cried over the phone and pleaded with me to walk away from it all.

Within a week of my release I had a car load of dockies looking for me and, unfortunately for them, they found me. But without the promised automatic weapons and hand grenades, I could not fully correct the situation.

In relation to the old Texan, the grand old man of the Melbourne criminal world, the wrong done to him at the hands of certain members of the union executive should not go unpunished. But had the automatic weapons been forthcoming, the 1977 dockies' Christmas party would have been a blast in every sense of the word, let me tell you.

Around that time a team of dockies were looking for me with a bag of lime and a shovel in the car. They found me, but I pulled out a meat cleaver and a sawn-off shotgun. They didn't even get out of the car; they just drove away with me laughing at them. Plastic gangsters.

Longley to me was in a way a second father, an uncle. If I had been Italian I'd call him my Godfather, not only a man of respect but a man I respect. In many ways the Overcoat Gang was there to protect old Billy, although old Bill never really knew it.

But it was generally known that any move towards Longley in Pentridge meant killing Chopper Read first, and whatever else I am, I'm not easily killed. The friendship between myself and Longley began in H Division labour yards in 1975–76. The enemy of my enemy is my friend. As a result we became friends and remain friends.

Longley was my mentor. He taught me tactics, strategy, patience, he taught me that one man can bring an army to its knees if he just watches and waits.

THE TEXAN

He's the man they love to hate,
Now they have him behind the gate,
Him and his team were dockland perfection,
They fought the Commies and won the election,
The other crew had to pull up their socks,
So they got Franny to pinch the box,
Pat and Putty said what a top plan,
But that's when the shit hit the fan,
The Pom was busy cutting toes,
The jacks sat back picking their nose,
The word was out the Texan had lost,
But nothing is gained without a cost,
A few broken heads and busted legs,
They were going down like bloody tent pegs,

Someone had a sweet connection,
There wasn't much police detection,
But when in doubt just blame the Texan,
Pat felt safe, it was his big day,
He even had a bodyguard,
But Machine Gun Bobby wasn't trying too hard,
The press roared like thunder,
Someone had to go under,
The other team had plenty to hide,
But the Crown Law gave them a nice free ride,
They couldn't beat him any other way,
So they loaded him up and sent him away.

William O'Meally

William John O'Meally was the last man legally flogged in Australia. He was convicted of killing police constable George Howell in 1952, and sentenced to death, but this was commuted to life in jail.

He was flogged for attempting to escape and spent 12 years of his 27-year sentence in solitary confinement.

O'Meally was portrayed as one of the toughest, most dangerous men in jail. He claimed he was 'the man they couldn't break' and stated he was behind prison riots and much of the violence inside Pentridge.

In later years O'Meally mellowed and became involved in writing poetry.

Although his papers were marked 'never to be released' he was freed in 1979.

Read remembers a very different O'Meally from the hard man image he had cultivated in prison over three decades.

One chap who had a big reputation but that I found very forgettable was Bill O'Meally. I first met him in B Division in 1975. He was an odd old chap with a sad complex about his hair falling out. He once tried to colour his grey hair with Nugget (shoe polish) and went out into the exercise yard to sunbake, but the sun was hot and he started to sweat. The Nugget began to run, and when he noticed it, he rushed off back into the division.

There are a host of people who have, in pride of place above the fireplace or in the dining room, an oil painting signed by William O'Meally. The fact is that any old crook who was in B Division when old Bill was there will tell you that Bill couldn't paint a fence with a spray can.

He soon gave up painting, but it didn't give him up ... jail is overcrowded with promising artists, all of them unknown and not able to sell their work for a good price. But with Bill's name on the bottom a painting could be sold for $1,200 or $1,500. Bill used to be called in to write his name on the bottom of various works of art.

Christ, I even sold an 'O'Meally' after it was given to me by a prisoner who owed me money.

The Pentridge painting trick was a great giggle. But there was a better one. At HM Prison Geelong the boys were turning out Pro Harts by the dozen, then sending them out to be sold as stolen property. No one was going to buy them if it was claimed they were legal, because buyers would have checked them and found they were fakes. But if it is a pile of two or three 'stolen' Pro Harts, then it's quite different. They can go for two or three grand each, bought by the greedy, stupid yuppie class.

It wasn't hard. Paints, canvas, paintbrushes, check out Pro Hart's style in an art book and away they went. Who's going to know the difference? It was a great old trick.

Greedy yuppies ... where would the crooks be without them? Coke, speed and hot property: they love it all.

Peter Lawless

Peter Lawless was one of the big names of crime in the 1970s. He was a star witness in the Beach Inquiry into the Police in 1975. Lawless was sentenced to life for the murder of Christopher Fitzgerald. In 1987 he was released after serving more than 14 years. He was then implicated in an attempted robbery of a National Australia bank in Ringwood later that year and sentenced to a further seven years.

Peter Lawless won't sue me. I'd punch his head in if he tried. I've known the bloke for 20 years; during the Overcoat Gang war in Pentridge he sat on the fence in H Division trying to be mates with both sides. He is a top jailhouse lawyer, nowhere near Peter Allen's level, but very skilled nevertheless.

Peter is known in jail as a non-tubber. In other words, he doesn't mind walking past the shower room, but not a lot of people can remember him stepping inside. He hasn't been seen taking his clothes off and hopping under the water.

There is a standing giggle in Pentridge and criminal circles that the only way for the police to get Peter Lawless to sign a confession is not to try threats of force or violence but to threaten him with a large bucket of hot, soapy water. It is said that Peter would sign his own granny up if he was threatened with the content of said bucket.

Of course, all this is said in jest, a bit of criminal mirth and comedy. However, all mirth and comedy is based on fact, and the fact is if a new prisoner asked Peter where the shower room was he would be in real trouble trying to offer the right directions.

Dave Dominguez

Dave Dominguez was a nice guy who fell victim to the modern epidemic of drug abuse. He was serving a short sentence for burglary when he died of a drug overdose in Pentridge's B Division. He was found dead in another prisoner's cell in April 1985. Heroin was found in his bloodstream, a puncture mark in his left arm. But no one ever found the syringe he was supposed to have used to inject himself.

Police said that a number of inmates refused to co-operate with their investigation into Big Dave's death.

'Big Dave' Dominguez was a six-foot two-inch, 22-stone lovable jolly giant who had befriended me in Geelong Prison in 1974. I spent 10 very happy months in that jail before being moved back to H Division, as it was thought I was standing over half the Geelong Prison.

It wasn't true. If fellow prisoners wish to give me money and gifts it would be impolite to refuse, and I'm nothing if not polite.

Big Dave, however, had a drug problem, and that problem almost created a falling-out between myself and my old friend Frankie Waghorn.

Big Dave would borrow money from other inmates and 'forget' to repay it. I would see to it that his debts were paid or cancelled. However, the drugs had taken their hold and Dave's word became totally worthless. I repaid his debts to the tune of several thousand dollars. It was only after I got out of jail in late 1984 that I came to understand that a large part of his friendship towards me was so he could stand behind my name, as he was a marked man.

His friendship with me was, in fact, keeping him alive. He got out of jail and used my name to borrow a further $1,150 from my girlfriend Margaret – and forgot to repay it. Eight weeks later he returned to Pentridge, to B Division. By this time I was again in H Division. He had blood enemies in B Division. On my final plea to repay Margaret, and his refusal, I withdrew my friendship and protection.

He was found dead in his cell of a drug overdose. That was in 1985.

Drugs have destroyed the lives, hearts and minds of too many good men. In my heart the memory of Big Dave still saddens me.

Johnny Morrison

John Lewis Morrison, like so many of his type, died a violent death. His remains were found by a sharefarmer in a crop of barley near Laverton in December 1972. He had been blasted in the head with a shotgun.

If God in heaven came down to earth and walked the streets of Melbourne under cover as a streetfighter he would not beat Johnny 'The Face' Morrison, even if God carried an axe. That is my opinion.

The Face got his nickname because he was an ugly bastard with a head full of pimples, boils and scars. He was befriended by my old dad. In fact, if the gossips and slander merchants who sometimes tease my dad because of me knew how many crazy streetfighters, killers and gunmen he has helped, they might be a tad more polite.

Morrison was murdered in the early 1970s in the dockies wars. He was found buried in a farmer's paddock at Werribee. But as a streetfighter in the 1960s 'The Face' was a blood and guts legend. He's forgotten now, and if I don't mention him he may never get a mention any place else. He held my coat for me when I was a young 14-year-old kid about to fight a much bigger and older boy with a big local reputation in Collingwood.

'The Face' said: 'Mark, reputations are based on a hundred facts – and a thousand fairytales. A horse is only as good as its last race. So get in there, rip his head off and piss down his neck.'

I lost the fight, but remembered the words. And I'll never forget 'The Face'. May he rest in peace.

Victor Frederick Allard

Victor Frederick Allard was one of the first Painters and Dockers to graduate to the drug world. A big man with a reputation as a standover man, he became a street heroin dealer and a well-known figure with the prostitutes in St Kilda.

In February 1979 Allard was shot dead, blasted three times in the stomach as he walked along Fitzroy Street.

He was in debt over heroin deals when he was murdered. His killing has not been solved.

Two years before he was murdered there had been another attempt on his life. He was shot in the stomach while drinking in a South Melbourne hotel in 1977.

There was one rat who smashed me over the head with an iron bar in St Kilda in late 1977. No wonder my memory is half shot to pieces, with the blows I've taken to the head over the years.

Vic Allard, the great fat hoon, was the one who smashed me over the head in the George Hotel. I punched and kicked the big wombat out of the pub and into the street, but he nearly killed me with the iron bar. I got terrible headaches for more that a year or so after that. Then Prison Officer Mick Millson smashed his baton over my head when Jimmy Loughnan and Johnny Price broke out of H Division in 1979 and climbed up on the A Division roof. Mick broke the baton over my head; he hit me between 15 to 20 times before it broke. I should thank him for it because after that, the headaches just stopped.

Allard was a dockie and some sort of crook, but mainly he was just a drunk who sold a bit of drugs.

The nitwit got himself murdered some time later in St Kilda.

Thomas Wraith

Thomas Wraith was a man with a reputation. He was involved in violent crime and drug distribution. He was suspected of killing a woman, Grace O'Connor, in England in the 1970s. Her body has never been found.

Wraith eventually lived in a de facto relationship with Mrs Rae Elizabeth Collingburn.

Mrs Collingburn was the wife of Keith Collingburn, a criminal who died after he had been in police custody in 1971. Two policemen were charged and acquitted of the manslaughter of Collingburn.

Wraith died in 1983 when repeatedly hit over the head with a tomahawk by Mrs Collingburn in their Brunswick home. She said Wraith had a gun and threatened to kill her. She said she had given him her pension cheque and some heroin.

Tommy Wraith was another two-bob gangster that Jimmy Loughnan got hold of in Pentridge during the 1970s.

We had him on his hands and knees barking like a dog. He had put a hole in his manners with Jimmy and despite Tommy's so-called tough reputation, with the help of me and my tomahawk, Tom was eager to get down on all fours and bark like a dog.

We sent him on his way with a moderate touch-up. Funny thing was he didn't have much luck with tomahawks. His wife chopped him to death as he slept in bed. She used a tomahawk too. Ha ha.

Robert Trimbole

Robert Trimbole was Australia's most wanted man. He was a key figure in the Griffith Mafia and wanted in connection with the murders of anti-drugs campaigner Donald Mackay and drug couriers Isabel and Douglas Wilson. He avoided arrest for years and died in Spain in 1987.

Anyone who has been to the Melbourne or Caulfield Cup would have seen Aussie Bob Trimbole standing in the betting ring with a fist full of money. Putting his bets on and losing heaps. I didn't know him but I had been introduced to him in the early 1970s. He struck me as a fat drunk and a man who was a born idiot and had lost ground ever since.

I think it was Vincent Villeroy who introduced me to Aussie Bob at the 1973 Caulfield Cup. He was introduced as a professional punter, but he looked more like a professional drinker. The fact that such a bum could climb the criminal ladder and have such financial power and pull is, in itself, proof positive that the Australian underworld could be flogged into total defeat by an angry troup of Girl Guides wielding tennis racquets.

When one considers Aussie Bob Trimbole, in the cold light of day, and looks at him logically, it is quite laughable. Why he was never grabbed and his shoe size shortened is beyond my power of understanding. From a drunk when I met him in 1973 to the Godfather of the Australia underworld. If Aussie Bob can do it, I shudder to think what the Japs can do once they set up shop here. For me, staying alive hasn't been too hard in the underworld. Dying of laughter has been my only real concern.

Chapter 24

An Unfortunate Life

'I'd rather die in bed in my own home of old age, than in a pool of blood in a cold concrete gutter in middle age.'

I HAVE survived dozens of murder attempts, three gang wars and Slim Minogue's jailhouse cooking. But I know that in the end, if I continue living as I always have, that I will end up being murdered. Death itself doesn't frighten me but I don't want to be shot in the back by some town drunk.

In the world of true blood and guts I am a big name, and I have walked over many bodies to get that reputation, but in the end, what does it all mean? Any one of those murder attempts against my good self could have killed me. I have had luck on my side. Don't get me wrong, I am not a reformed character who has found God. I don't weep for my fallen opponents. As far as I am concerned the world is a better place without them, as they were all scum. But I am a man who knows that his luck cannot run forever. The fact that I have lived as long as I have is an indictment on the mental and physical abilities of my enemies.

At the moment I am working towards my third generation of enemies, *Miami Vice*-style police and plastic yuppy gangsters with car phones and coke habits, who call themselves crooks. None of them ever intend to face each other on the field of combat. Bugger them all, that is why I want to go home, go to Tasmania and leave them all to destroy themselves.

If I remained in the world of crime where I have been for 20 years I would be spitting in the face of my own logic. I've read military tactics and strategy all my life; to walk away and never look back is the smart move. It is the only logical tactic left to me − for every Napoleon there is a Wellington. I intend to walk away before I find myself in the field of combat at my own Waterloo. To do otherwise would be to ignore a lifetime of study. When a man starts lying to himself he is finished. I am no longer as physically big, strong or as fast as I once was. It is true that I have forgotten more shifty tricks than 1000 crooks would learn in a lifetime. However, what happened to Wild Bill Hickock sticks in my mind. And, as they say, Jesse James was shot in the back by Charlie Ford, the coward of the county.

My life is a spinning coin: heads I die, tails I lose, and the coin hasn't landed yet. Tactics tell me to get to safe ground before it does. I'd rather die in bed in my own home of old age, than in a pool of blood in a cold concrete gutter in middle age.

There are those who will not believe me, those who think

it is an elaborate subterfuge and that I will return to the mainland to wage war. But that would be to ignore one important fact – if I do not change my ways I have only jail and death in my future. There will always be someone who wants to kill me, because I have made too many enemies over the years. There are too many men who fear the name Chopper Read, and a frightened man is a dangerous one.

The gung-ho types that get around armed to the teeth, the big tough fellows who go to the gymnasium and have half a dozen black belts and bulging biceps and walk around with a knife in their teeth, they're no problem. You can see them coming a mile away.

It's the quiet, insipid little rat of a character who sneaks around the place, lurking outside with his little sawn-off .22 and dreams of blowing away Chopper Read and getting his name in the paper. That's the one to look for.

Think about it. The bloke who kills me can write his own ticket. He would never have to buy another beer for the rest of his life. There would be pubs he could walk into where he could get a counter lunch and a beer forever. There would be massage parlors in Melbourne where they would write his name on the wall and say if this man enters here he is to pay nothing. There would be Italians who would get pizza shop owners to provide this man with pizzas until he could eat no more. Free sex, beer and food until he was old and grey.

What choice have I got. I have to bail out.

I'm not 26 any more, and I feel about 66. You don't age

gracefully in jail. I've got more injuries than the average 60-year-old man. You spend 18 hours a day locked in a cell. I've spent 10 years in H Division, and there are blokes who come down here and scream their heads off after two nights. I was the first prisoner who ever set foot in Jika Jika. I spent three years there. So that's 13 years maximum security, and some people reckon that wasn't enough. That's not to mention the rest of the jail I've done. And it's not as if I do relaxed prison, because there is always someone to watch out for. There is always someone with his eye on Chopper. It's the same on the outside. I can't stand at a bar and have a relaxed beer; I can't sit in a restaurant and have a relaxed meal.

Life gives you two choices, you either cry your bloody eyes out, or laugh your head off. The thing is, I've got nothing to laugh about, but I refuse to cry. You have to see the funny side of some very black situations. But if you were to really look at my life, at what I have done and what I have become, there is nothing to laugh about.

There are young men who look up to crooks and criminal identities; I know I did when I was younger. But to all the up and comers out there with hearts full of dreams and heads full of shit about criminal glory, there are some bad old boys out there watching and waiting for blokes like you. When you've made enough money from the drugs and climbed high enough up the ladder to be worth the bother, one night someone will be waiting.

You will be in a crowded nightclub in your expensive

clothes, with gold jewellery and a gun in your pocket. You will have a couple of chicks on your arm, plenty of cash in your pocket and you will not sense the danger. You will be feeling on top of the world when you walk out into the early morning air to catch a cab or walk to your posh car ... that's when some mad smiling psycho will walk up behind you and tap your shoulder.

When the gas bottle is lit, it will be too late to walk away. And if the bloke has curly hair, big blue eyes and no front teeth then, young fella, you are in big trouble. All you can do is give him what he wants and plead for a quick death. The bloke doing the job won't be me and he may not have my medical expertise; you may even bleed to death before you can make a deal. Either way, if you call that criminal glory, you're madder than I am. You won't like the smell of your own feet burning. No-one ever does.

To all the parents and teachers who want to punch their personal beliefs down the necks of the children, be careful.

To the police, never get so arrogant and self-confident that you think you are the smartest cop in Melbourne.

To all the bullies in the school yard, the little boy you pick on today may not be the same little kid tomorrow.

To all the kids who read gangster books and go to gangster movies – don't get involved in real life. If you do then one day you may lose your life.

To the kids who think that going to jail will make you tough, consider this. Only every 10 or 20 years does a really tough one come along. The rest of you will only be bare bums in the shower watching your backs.

To the judges: don't forget that you all started as lawyers and each of you fought and lost cases convinced your client was an innocent man. Not everyone who steps into the dock is guilty.

To the young cub reporters, the police media liaison office is not the burning bush or the Holy Grail. Get out into the streets, the pubs and the racetracks and find out yourself.

And to the crims who think they are better than the rest, so was Wild Bill Hickock and you know what happened to him. Shot in the back by the town drunk.

I will reveal something no-one knows. In Jika Jika in 1987 before the fire, I got punched on the jaw when I wasn't paying attention and knocked to the floor by a pool, a jail poof. The fact that the offender now lives his life in constant fear is beside the point. The point is that Mark Brandon 'Chopper' Read – one of the meanest, treacherous, bloodiest bits of work to emerge in the Melbourne underworld this century – got decked by a two bob poof. There is no excuse. I dropped my guard. And one day it could be a bullet instead of a fist, and I don't want my tombstone to read: 'Here lies Chopper Read, shot by a drunk when he wasn't looking'.

I could tell a hundred stories of violence that in the end would mean nothing. Inside jail I have come face to face with the fact that my life, the sum total of my life, has been a wasted effort.

Since I was 20 I have been on the outside for about 13 months. The rest of the time has been spent doing jail. It hasn't been a good life, it's just been a bloody waste.

I've done nothing. When was the last time I saw a sunset or took the time to be normal? The only time I can remember relaxing was on the plane ride from Launceston to Melbourne. I could enjoy the ride. I now want to be able to walk away and for the first time, relax. All I have ever had is tension and stress.

To live a life where there has always been violence, attacks against me and hatred has finally gotten to me. I have friends that go back 20 years but in the end, I always end up alone in a prison cell. I don't want to be an old man with a ripping yarn to tell. I want to live a life that is a little normal.

It is time to leave the criminal world and try and salvage something in my remaining years so that it is not all a waste.

I know I have said that I regret nothing – but the truth is that I regret plenty. I regret my whole life. I regret not continuing at school. I regret spending half my life behind bars. I regret not spending more time with my dear old Dad. I regret my poor Margaret having to suffer the torment of having to visit me in jail for eight years. I regret the sad deaths of some true and loyal boyhood friends who died because I, in my blood lust, ordered them into street battles they could never win. I regret that in my single-minded madness to get at my enemies that some non-combatants have fallen by the wayside.

I regret not having lived a real life, not being able to walk the streets of the city I love without having to look over my shoulder. Every time I sit down, it has to be with my back to the wall and facing the door.

I regret that once you've built a reputation in the criminal world you have two choices: die or vanish. I regret that all the grand old fellows I have mentioned in this book never bothered to pull my coat and never bothered to explain to me the real horror of it all.

I regret that I have not been close to my mother or sister. I regret the death of Cowboy Johnny, who took a broken bottle in the neck to save my life.

To the young blokes out there who look up to me, and I know there are a few of you sneaking around, stay at school. And if you have made up your minds to be gangsters, then get yourself a briefcase and become a gangster in the boardrooms of the nation, because that's how the real gangsters do it.

Je ne regrette rien. 'I regret nothing.' What a sick joke. I regret everything.